A MAN
OF HIGH
CHARACTER

A MAN OF HIGH CHARACTER

HOW AND WHY
A CHRISTIAN SHOULD LIVE

MITCHELL WHITE

Wonderful Life
Publishing

A MAN OF HIGH CHARACTER
HOW AND WHY A CHRISTIAN SHOULD LIVE

First published 2019

Cover design by Ryan Forsythe

Original Image by Dimitris Vetsikas from Pixabay

ISBN: 9781711791425

Contents

PREFACE

Why should we bother striving for great things when we are unable to understand the meaning of life? Should we bother learning new perspectives if we already have an adequate perspective on life? Should we trust our spouse if we have been told they are cheating?

These questions, and many more, can be ignored, but they ought to be wrestled with so that we are prepared for such circumstances if they should arise.

This book details the philosophy that a man of high character holds. This book was not written for those who want to fall between the cracks and fade away. It was written for those who want to understand what it truly means to become virtuous and transcend the basic norms that too many follow without thinking. It is for those who desire to solve problems that others do not dare meddle with, to have relationships that flourish, to be a fierce beast with passion and a rational intellect filled with persistence, aiming at something worthwhile. This is a book for those who desire to be a man of high character.

This is your warning: this book proposes ideas rarely taught in our society. I will apply common sense but stray from the common thought.

For some, this will only irritate, as it will feel like I am throwing a wrench in their belief system. Others may pick up the wrench and fine-tune their belief system.

While I tend to refer to men, this book is equally applicable to women. Though it may seem isolating, the title of the book comes from the root of the word "virtue" and it is not meant to exclude anyone.

Furthermore, I will be upfront in saying that I am religious, particularly Christian. While this book is for everyone, I will compare and contrast some religious ideas to the virtues discussed in each chapter. Even those who are not religious will benefit from the core ideas regarding how to be a man of high character.

To those who have picked up this book, I must commend you. You are not blindly living as the person society has prescribed you to be but, instead, are pursuing and daring to become something greater.

Mitchell White

CHAPTER I

"Virtue itself turns vice, being misapplied;
And vice sometimes by action dignified."
- William Shakespeare[1]

Understanding Virtues

We have all heard it said that patience and courage are virtues; yet, we neglect the fact that anger too is a virtue. We avoid calling anger, selfishness and jealousy virtues because it is easier to put them in a group of bad characteristics that should be avoided at all costs. Despite the fact that it is easier to categorize them negatively, the truth remains that these traits are virtues.

If the opening statement has offended or confused you, then we must spend time understanding what virtue is. I did not say that anger is good; I merely called it a virtue. Perhaps, you have mistakenly assumed that virtues are always good. All virtues have a time when they are moral and a time when they are immoral.

Patience and courage are virtues, but does that mean they are always the ideal characteristics to exhibit?

When someone runs off with your child, should you be patient? No. When I offer you a vial of poison and tell you to be brave and drink it, should you be courageous and drink it? No. If you believe that virtues are meant to be absolutely good, such as patience and courage, then your ideology of blindly following specific virtues will periodically result in foolish and unwise decisions.

We have been told to possess certain virtues, regardless of the circumstances. However, circumstances matter, as the world is not distinctly black and white. To blindly pursue specific virtues is not righteous. Blindly pursuing virtues is a flawed ideology that the world will gladly use to its advantage in politics, business or conversation.

We all ought to be capable of patience, courage, love and faith, but that does not mean we should always exhibit each of those virtues. In the same way, we ought to be capable of jealousy, anger, pride and selfishness, but that does not mean we should always exhibit these virtues.

The purpose of this book is to teach you how to best handle your God-given abilities so that you can be properly equipped to live to your full potential. The aim is to equip you with the knowledge to live as righteously as you can so that you can properly face the chaos in your life and optimally pursue what is meaningful and worthwhile.

Etymology of Virtue

The word *virtue* originates from the Romans. The Romans began with the Latin word *vir*, which means *Man*, and then evolved the word *vir* to form the word *virtutem,* which means to have moral strength, high character, goodness, manliness, valor, bravery, excellence and worth. The Latin word *virtutem* was then translated into Old French as *vertu*. Finally, in the 13th century, the word *vertu* was borrowed from Old French by the English and called *virtue,* which is the word we use today.[2]

Essentially, a *virtue* is a trait or quality that a man of high character may exhibit at any time. To be *virtuous* means to conduct oneself in the way *a man of high character* would.

With that in mind, we must then determine what a man of high character does. Does a man of high character get angry or bestow wrath upon others? Or should he always be kind and gentle? A great man is not angry all the time, but when he is, his anger is righteous and proper. Yet, very few consider anger to be a virtue. We prefer to promote virtues, such as peace and kindness, that are generally the right characteristic to exhibit. A man of high character is peaceful and kind during times of civility, but what about in a time of war? Was

George Washington not a man of high character because he led an army and did not promote peace during the revolution?

We often only look at the behavior of great men when times are civil and tranquil and tell society that we should emulate those characteristics. We do not particularly enjoy dwelling on the darker times, where other virtues are the proper characteristics to exhibit. We seldom ponder the shadows and valleys where we may one day find ourselves.

We don't want to imagine a world where we have to be jealous because our love might decide to love someone else. Yet, the Christian God is a jealous God and is someone Christians believe to possess highly regarded characteristics. The Bible commands Christians to "*be imitators of God*" (Ephesians 5:1)[3]. We promote peace and tell others to let go of their anger. Nonetheless, the Christian God has exhibited anger towards those who abuse widows and entire nations that did evil. Jesus became angry and turned over tables in the temple. Even so, many Christians live by an ideology where jealousy and anger are considered immoral.

You must understand the benefits and consequences of each virtue as well as the proper and improper time to exhibit each virtue. We need more than a blind ideology of following just one virtue or following a rigid hierarchy of virtues. We need rational people who understand virtues and how to be virtuous.

We must understand that all virtues have circumstances in which they are good and when they are also not ideal characteristics to exhibit. For example, *courage* is the proper virtue when faced with a daunting task. However, if we should not participate in the task, then it is ideal to *discourage* ourselves from participating. Likewise, anger is *often* not the right characteristic to exhibit, but a man of high character should be angry when the proper circumstance presents itself.

ANGER

Aristotle said that there is a time and a circumstance for anger, but few men know when it is appropriate.

> "*Anyone can get angry – that is easy… but to do this with the right person, to the right extent, at the right time, with the*

5

right motive, and in the right way, that is not for everyone, nor is it easy."
- Aristotle[4]

Given the nature of virtues, you can replace the word *angry* with any virtue in this statement.

Perhaps, it is easier to find examples of anger being bad and courage being good, leading us to teach the young that anger is bad in general and to stay away from it because they are not smart enough to know the proper time to be angry. The truth is that not all people are smart enough or capable enough to truly understand the full context of when to utilize each virtue. This is why we teach children the virtues that are generally good to give them easy-to-follow guidance in the beginning. But we should aim to help children grow into men who are capable of living virtuously and right in every regard. As we become capable of comprehending virtues and circumstances, we ought to leave behind the childish ideologies and aim for righteousness. Yet, many avoid this responsibility and stick to the basics that are easy to digest.

"For though by this time you ought to be teachers, you need someone to teach you again the basic principles of the oracles of God. You need milk, not solid food, for everyone who lives on milk is unskilled in the word of righteousness, since he is a child. But solid food is for the mature, for those who have their powers of discernment trained by constant practice to distinguish good from evil."
- Hebrews 5:12–14

You are an adult who should have grown up and become capable of understanding when each virtue should be properly exhibited. You ought to know when loyalty is good and when loyalty is evil. You ought to know when anger is good and when anger is evil. The greater man develops his character and becomes knowledgeable of what is good and evil so that he may be virtuous and aim for righteousness. The weaker man clings to childish ideologies where anger is absolutely bad and courage is always good; sacrificing righteousness for simplicity.

"Be angry, and do not sin."

- Psalm 4:4

TOOLS

We can choose to engage in the idea of being virtuous, which is doing as a man of high character would, but this comes with its risks. When you decide that anger is appropriate at times, it opens you up the possibility that you might be able to exhibit anger at an inappropriate time. It takes training and understanding, which some of us might find difficult, to dare to become virtuous. That is why we start small and take on more as we can.

Anger is a ferocious wolf that often destroys those who engage with it. It is often terrible and destructive, so we shun it completely. A wolf is often shot and killed because most say that it has no chance of being tamed. However, to a great tamer of animals, the wolf might be domesticated, and after an extended period of time, the wolf can become your best friend, greatest ally and weapon. Just because something is dangerous that does not mean we should consider it inherently evil. German shepherds are one of the most aggressive breeds of dogs, and yet they are the most useful in wartime.

Yes, virtues can be devastating when used improperly, and I believe it is sinful and reprehensible to use them when not appropriate, but in the appropriate circumstance, they can be a powerful tool for good.

I want to liken anger to a dangerous tool. It can hurt many if we give it to everyone. Many will say that it can cut a man in half and kill him, and they are right. But sometimes, we need a dangerous tool in a drastic situation to stop a terrible power. Sometimes, such a large tool is needed to end a war. Sometimes, it's needed to get through to an irrational person before they cause mayhem. It can be useful in good hands. So, do not say that we should ban the tool; instead, say that we need to create men who understand how to use the tool properly and virtuously. That ought to be our aim!

Some will say that we should just stick to the tools we know are fairly safe. If a house needs to be constructed, using a chisel to cut down trees might keep everyone safe, but is clearly not optimal. Let us learn to wield a chainsaw properly so that the work is completed efficiently and does not waste time. We have been given great tools and it would be a shame to say that we will forever be too childlike to utilize them. We will be holding ourselves back if we do so.

You need to develop and obtain tools to aid you because life is not easy and pleasant. You will have to face problems and challenges. And it is best to obtain the tools that will best help you solve our relative problems. If you need to attach two pieces of wood together, then equip yourself with a hammer. If you need to become angry and put your body in the *fight-or-flight* state to chase down someone who is kidnapping your children, then learn how to wield anger and use it properly. Kindness and patience are not ideal in such a situation. It is best to have an equipped self. It is better to be capable and armed and dangerous and virtuous than to be stripped naked and defenseless and have no power to make any difference in this world.

Therefore, do not shoot the ferocious *wolves of anger* and let the *dogs of courage* meander everywhere because they seem harmless and good-natured most of the time. Know when to use each and when to leave them in the kennel. Sometimes, you may be too small and incapable of training certain virtues; then start with the small ones and learn to become a master of yourself by proceeding with one virtue at a time.

You must choose your suffering and discomfort when it is in the pursuit of something worthwhile. You can suffer when life comes at you and beats you down because you are weak and defenseless, or you can choose to undergo a difficult period of training now, when things are decently pleasant, by understanding how to use these tools or virtues that can be used to defend and attack.

You can choose to be nothing and have nothing and pose little risk to the world. Or you can think and engage in the natural, God-given conscience you were bestowed with and think about how to properly use the tools at your disposal. Do not waste your conscience and follow norms and rules blindly; think, prepare, engage the beasts when you are capable, train them and allow their ferocity to be in your capacity, so that when the proper moment to unleash them presents itself, you are well-equipped to handle the challenge.

Many declare that you should be an *individual*, but they often cannot describe what it means to be an *individual*. I believe that being an *individual* means trying to understand the proper way to conduct yourself by using your conscience, by engaging with your natural, God-given gifts. Become the master of yourself and the virtues, not a slave to society by ridding yourself of everything that may protect you.

But I must say, there is comfort in following other peoples' ideologies. It is easy and potentially could be better than your current belief system. For example, many partake in diet plans that will tell them exactly what to do and what to eat for a short period of time. For a person living an unhealthy lifestyle, this diet plan may create great results but often all of the benefits are lost after the diet ends. If the dieter never understands calories and why they are eating different foods on the diet, then they doom themselves in the long run when the short term diet ends. It is not wrong to join a group when you have little understanding of what to do, but aim to become autonomous and to determine for yourself what is good and bad.

Intuitiveness is rarely encouraged, for there is power in telling others what to do. If you are dependent on me to make your decisions, then I can impose a cost upon you. But if you learn how to think and how to act properly, then you will no longer need me, and I will have no power over you. I cannot extort you for money or attention. We want others to be dependent on us so that we can continue to thrive off their incompetence and unwillingness to be a conscience individual.

Obviously, there are some who present a diet plan and teach others how to have a mindful connection with their eating habits, but those people are in the minority. The majority of consumers want convenience and to be told what is right and what is wrong in the short term. They want to replace the strict rules their parents have given them with a new set of strict rules and pretend it is their own. Therefore, the market is filled with suppliers who prescribe you a plan and send you on your way so you keep coming back to them. It is as if you have adopted new parents. Learn the principles from your parents and from others, but then begin to think for yourself when you are capable of bearing such a burden.

A Circuit Breaker

When I imagine virtues, I do not see them in a hierarchy with honesty at the top and the other virtues below. Instead, I visualize each of the virtues on a circuit breaker panel. In every home, there is a circuit breaker panel, containing a handful of switches that are either switched on or off, which determine how to distribute the electrical power to different energy sources in a home. Each virtue is like a switch that can be turned on or off depending on the circumstance.

Some say that honesty is always the reigning champion that should always trump all other virtues, but this doesn't seem to be the case to me. There are times when the truth needs to be restrained. If I ask for your bank account information, is it right to be truthful and transparent and give it to me? No. This does not mean that one should break the trust of another person but merely refrain from telling the truth. Sometimes, the ideal responses are *"You need to figure it out yourself;" "I am not at liberty to tell you;" "I don't think I should tell you the truth because you will not use it for good;"* or *"We will tell you that when you are old enough to understand."*

To show that a hierarchy of virtuous actions should not be the ideal structure to determine our daily actions, I will provide an example. Is it better to be courageous and stand up for your rights or to be merciful and let another person impede upon your rights? Those possessing a mindset that utilizes a hierarchy might say it is nobler to stand up for your rights and bring justice to anyone who impedes. But when we look at a real-life example, it does not always appear that having a rigid hierarchy is ideal. For example, if you are driving and someone is cutting in line when lanes are merging together, do you defend your rights to go first and risk crashing your car to stand up for your rights? They might be a jerk, or they might not be paying attention or having an emergency. Is it worth it? I would think that in most cases of driving, it is not worth crashing, and it may be wise in some circumstances to concede your right to go first.

What if your government is taking away your freedom of speech? Do you grant the government the right to take your right away or do you stand up and defend yourself? I would think that in most cases, it is worth standing up and defending your rights. Therefore, a simple hierarchy that you can apply to all things is not the ideal.

We cannot react strictly based on certain values. If you visualize the virtues as a circuit panel, you have the right to send the power to any of the virtues or to cut it off, but you do not have to do something immoral.

You may choose to exhibit or refrain from exhibiting each virtue based on what you think a man of high character would do.

VIRTUOUS

I am not very fond of the idea that "*If you have nothing nice to say, say nothing at all.*" This phrase puts forth the idea that kindness is always more important than truth. Sometimes, the truth needs to be said even when it can hurt others' feelings. Let's look at two examples. If you are in your home, then it is wrong for me to come into your house and tell you that you are unhealthy and should change your lifestyle. However, if you put yourself in a situation that declares yourself as capable of handling the truth, then expect the truth from others. If you go to school, the teacher can grade your assignments. If you go to work, your boss will review you and you should expect honesty over kindness.

The idea of placing kindness over truth, which comes from the film *Bambi*, may be a good philosophy for a child who is not wise enough to know when others are subject to and in need of the truth, but you are an adult and should have a more refined philosophy. Sometimes we should be gentle when dealing with something that may easily break beyond the point that is beneficial for growth. Sometimes roughness is ideal when something ought to be dealt with harshly in order to stimulate growth.

It is virtuous to exhibit confidence when you are competent in a subject. It is improper to be confident when you are uncertain of your competence or you know that you are not an expert. To be confident about the future is often perceived as arrogance because no one truly knows the future.

For so long, we have taught that you should not be prideful but humble. And because people blindly follow the virtue of humility, the pendulum has swung too far to one side. Now, some have realized that telling people that they should be proud of themselves would make the receiver have some pride in themselves and feel motivated to pursue their dreams. To capitalize on the movement, some teachers have begun teaching the idea that *you are enough*. You are capable and should always be proud. They give anecdotal examples about how a celebrity or hard-working person was putting too much pressure on themselves and was taught to never be prideful, so they stayed away from ever believing in themselves of accomplishing something great. Then, teachers preach the idea that everyone should be proud of themselves, even when they have nothing to be proud of or are incapable of handling a dangerous task.

They switch from one virtue to the next. From humility to pride. From pride back to humility after everyone makes a fool of themselves and is unable to accomplish a feat. Yet, rarely is the message taught that each virtue is appropriate sometimes, and inappropriate at others. Instead of telling the truth, they set up two camps that battle it out, the war gathers attention, and the preachers win while the followers become casualties. They do not teach that there is a time for love, hate, war and peace.

> *"A time to weep, and a time to laugh;*
> *a time to mourn, and a time to dance;*
> *a time to cast away stones, and a time to gather stones together;*
> *a time to embrace, and a time to refrain from embracing;*
> *a time to seek, and a time to lose;*
> *a time to keep, and a time to cast away;*
> *a time to tear, and a time to sew;*
> *a time to keep silence, and a time to speak;*
> *a time to love, and a time to hate;*
> *a time for war, and a time for peace."*
> - Ecclesiastes 3:4–8

So, investigate each virtue. Learn the proper times to exhibit each one so you can have the wisdom to properly wield it when the time comes.

Take some time to consider the virtues you are capable of and then ponder the circumstances dictating when each virtue is appropriate and inappropriate. Understand when it is proper to have desires, seek attention, love and hate, release, speak, listen, wage war, act rationally and act based on your passions or emotions.

Imagine if we held our politicians to these standards. We ought to ask them when they think are the appropriate circumstances for going to war, to create regulations and to fund a public project.

LEARN TO BE VIRTUOUS

To play the guitar, sometimes you just have to start playing. By playing, you can hear what sound each movement creates. You can retain what is beautiful and try to stop making mistakes when they occur. Learning the chords without an instrument can be of great value, but no one ever became a master musician by only understanding the theory. You may learn and read books, but at some point, you need to play. Likewise, you may learn what is right and virtuous, but you will only be great if you practice these virtues and aim to do them properly.

Therefore, learn and play. Aim for proper virtuousness and practice so that notes are properly played, and you no longer make mistakes during the easy songs. Later, when you no longer fail during the difficult songs, then you can attempt the extraordinary. *You may still fail, but even at that point, you sound beautiful to those who have not played at all.* And with enough practice and pursuit of the goal, you will accomplish the extraordinary.

You must teach yourself and your young how to be virtuous. One virtue at a time. Start with the ones that are usually good, like courage, and teach them how to properly exhibit it and show them the positive benefits. Teach them when it is proper and when it's improper to exhibit the virtue. After it is understood, move on to other virtues. It's best to start with ones that are almost always good because those are easy to understand. I would not mention *proper anger* until they are smart enough to know when the rare circumstances arise and if they are capable of doing it properly with a genuine desire for good.

If you don't teach virtues properly, others will prey on the weak and take advantage of those who lack an understanding. In 1935, the Nazi government released a propaganda film titled *Triumph of the Will*, to show the power of the German state two decades after the First World War. In the video, the youth of Germany are summoned, to which thousands upon thousands respond, to attend a speech by Adolf Hitler himself. Hitler speaks to the mass and says, "*We want our people to love peace, but also to be brave. And you must be peace-loving... [long pause for applause]... And so, you must be peace-loving and courageous at the same time.*"[5]

Being a notorious dictator and reviled man, I found his speech confusing. Why was Hitler encouraging the youth, who would be Nazi soldiers in the future, to "*love peace*"? This was not the Hitler I was taught about in school, and it was not the image of Hitler we try to plaster on rising politicians when they express extreme views. I expected a man who preached hate and advocated the murder of innocents. But reality shows that Hitler was preaching virtues while using words like *love* because he was smart and manipulative. Those are the real tyrants you ought to be afraid of. He would need them to be focused on being courageous and do whatever it takes to obtain the picture of *peace* that he had painted, regardless of the circumstance.

Hitler knew that youth have always been inspired by heroic and brave men who blazed trails before them. Knowing this, he would tell them they need to be *courageous* if they wanted to be proper citizens. And then he would play to their *loyalty*. Hitler went on to say, "*You are the flesh of our flesh and the blood of our blood.*" He gained their trust. He assumed the role of the loving father who was wise and had obedient children. During the speech, he declared many times that the youth must be obedient. He desired two virtues more than any other—courage and loyalty.

Courage to march into battle and loyalty to blindly follow Hitler. He did not teach them when it was proper to be loyal or when it was proper to be courageous. He convinced them to do his dirty work by encouraging them to blindly chase virtues.

Malicious tyrants are able to use the unwise. They will refrain from using those who think for themselves because their antics will be called out. Learning how to be virtuous will not only prevent you from being used by tyrannical powers but will also deter them from attempting to be tyrannical over you.

Too often young people are brainwashed into supporting certain companies or programs because they are told that doing so means that they are courageous, brave and loyal. I am not saying that these virtues are inherently bad, but we must know when to deny loyalty.

As a student of economics, I find it shocking to see people walk into these multi-level marketing traps (pyramid schemes). But it's no wonder they do. These companies are smart. They don't sell you products and the truth; they sell virtues that you have been taught to obey. They do not display the product, but display the virtues needed to pursue *their* desires. They preach that you should always be *courageous* and join their company. That if you have enough *faith* in yourself, you will succeed. And we fall for it because we hear that we should be courageous and faithful, which is associated with good, so we jump in headfirst because we are aiming for what we think is good. Then, they sell you shackles to cuff yourself, and you are told to have the courage to put them on. They sell you poison to drink, and you courageously obey to prove your *loyalty*.

"And there are others who are like cheap clocks that must be wound: they tick and they want the tick-tock to be called virtue. Verily, I have my pleasure in theses: wherever I find such clocks, I shall wind and wound them with my mockery, and they shall whir for me."

- Friedrich Nietzsche[6]

If we do not obtain a balanced and accurate understanding of virtues, then one of two realities will manifest. One is that specific actions will be required of you because certain virtues are considered absolutely good, such as loyalty and courage. The government or the majority will determine what you must or must not do, depriving you of your independence and freedom. Or society will begin to dislike and hate anyone who properly uses a virtue that has a negative preconceived notion. At first, the ones that are most often negative will go, such as anger, hate and selfishness. Then, they will take more virtues away, such as intelligence and strength, as these are sometimes good but can be used improperly. Towards the end, they will demonize honesty, trust, childbearing and love, leaving us barely even human at all. Either option leads to dehumanization.

Make yourself the person who is capable of each virtue. Make yourself the person who can handle the truth when it is given. Make yourself the person who is capable of being calm and patient, who can fight with strength, who can forgive, who can solve difficult problems and who can love with passion. That does not mean we should always do these things, but we should aim to be capable.

God didn't give us anger so that we can sin. No. Anger is a virtue. Anger builds up our adrenaline and allows us to confront evil or harm when used properly. We ought to say that anger is a virtue! That does not mean the virtue is always good or always bad. We ought to learn the circumstances in which it is proper to be angry so that we can act like a man of high character. That is what it means to be virtuous.

Unconditional

When you tell me something or someone is hateful, it is not enough for me to think lowly of the hate, as it can be justified and good. When you tell me something is capable of evil, that is not enough for it to be illegal, as we should not limit our ability to be virtuous. When you tell me that someone is trying to persuade you by inspiring fear, that is not enough for me to dislike the person because fear can be justified. When you tell me that someone is courageous, that is not enough for me to approve the action as they may be misguided. When you tell me that someone is mean, I will ask if the mean actions are warranted.

Life is not so black and white. The great life requires thought. It requires studying and understanding. Do not be simple-minded and see certain actions as always good and bad. Look at the world and do as the ideal man would do.

But that is difficult as we like simple ideas that are easy to follow. We love the simplicity of a linear plan that never changes. We embrace simple ideologies as if they were absolute truth. We either advocate going to one extreme or always being in moderation. We do not tell people to think. We advocate burning the boats and attacking. We advocate disregarding any thought towards a plan B because it might distract from plan A. And I agree that if you don't have the discipline to attack without your fear paralyzing you when you need courage, then plan B would be detrimental as you are unable to maintain plan A and plan B at the same time.

But a great man develops the discipline to ferociously attack, while he still has the boats onshore in case a retreat is necessary. The greater man aims for plan A but keeps a plan B in case his primary plan fails. He is able to have the discipline to focus on plan A despite plan B being available. The greater man is able to think about what is ideal and choose it amongst many options.

Do not aim to be so simple minded that you must restrict yourself from the ideal situation because it makes one option easier to focus on. Aim for the ideal and develop the capabilities to handle it properly.

Still, we love simplicity. If we do not endorse doing one thing to an extreme, we endorse doing *everything in moderation*. What a childlike idea! This idea is only ever used to justify your bad behaviors that you know you should stay away from. No one says, "*I haven't had any exercise this week. Well, I guess all things should be in moderation and therefore I should go exercise.*" No, they say *all things in moderation* and partake in that which they know they ought not to do.

Deep down, we know that all things have their place and time. However, we are too lazy to sort them out and just say that a little bit of everything is adequate. We know drugs are useful sometimes and destructive at other times, but instead of determining the times in which they are useful, we just take them in moderation at any time. Perhaps, we use that theory to justify our shortcomings or we say it because we would rather be lazy than using our conscience.

We ought to say, "*All good things in moderation and avoid that which is bad for you.*" For even the things that are good at one point can be overdone and become bad. Eating an apple is usually good but eating the 1,000th apple in a sitting will surely cause more harm than good. Thus, when something is good for you, partake in moderation or until it becomes bad. When it is bad for you, abstain. This should be common knowledge, yet I still hear the old adage, "*Everything in moderation.*"

These ideas are not new. William Shakespeare was able to deliver these concepts all with one noble character in Romeo and Juliet. The Friar Laurence wisely tells Romeo that he ought to "*love moderately; long love doth so; too swift arrives as tardy as too slow.*"[7] He understood that a reckless love without consideration might cause one to kill oneself.

The friar also understood how virtues are to be viewed. As he looked at the flower that contained the poison Juliet would drink, he remarked, "*Virtue itself turns vice, being misapplied; and vice sometimes by action dignified.*"[1] The friar did not look at poison with complete avoidance for it could be used properly for good. He also knew that love could be deadly if done irrationally. Shakespeare was showing us that everything could be good or bad, depending on the circumstances.

What else is a good story, other than the display of reality and consequences for us to learn from? What else is good music, other than a conversation with the most eloquent of orators? What else is good art, other than the deliverance of a philosophy? What else is a man of high character, other than one who understands virtues and chooses to live virtuously?

If there is anything to learn from great artists, it is that the ideal man is rare and, yet, we are all capable of becoming him. We need only to be daring enough to aim at being virtuous. We must dare to understand the proper time for anger, jealousy, forgiveness, fear, love and all other virtues and choose to live virtuously as a man of high character.

"When you forgive, you in no way change the past—but you sure do change the future."
- Bernard Meltzer[1]

Fortunately Forgiving

Forgiving and Bitterness

I don't know whether we forgive too much or too little, but I do know that we often do it without properly considering when we should forgive. We preach the idea of unconditional forgiveness far too often. I am not against forgiveness; it is simply that I am for forgiveness only under the proper circumstances.

The idea of unconditional forgiveness is taught widely in the Christian church and by gurus, hoping to relieve us of the bitterness and burdens we have been carrying. They teach that people ought to forgive others' wrongdoings immediately, completely and regardless of what the offender has done. But is that what the Bible really teaches?

Our culture often focuses only on the times that we should forgive because those are pleasant and happy times.

A question we ought to ask is this: *Why do we need to forgive?* As a child, I remember being at a church camp where a pastor spoke at length about forgiving people in our hearts and letting go of the burden. I remember watching as people cried and later testified that they felt like a weight had been lifted off them. The joy others received from forgiving filled the room. Afterward, they were able to reconnect with those they had forgiven. The metaphorical wall between them had crumbled to the ground when it was hit with the conviction of forgiveness. I saw, firsthand, people coming together in a way that allowed for growth and fellowship. Forgiveness can be a beautiful thing if done right because it can lead to reconciliation and peace.

We need other people in our lives and forgiveness allows us to retain relationships. We will have times when we are sick, weak and beaten down and we need another to take care of us for a period of time. Other people can help provide a new perspective on projects or offer a unique trait that is valuable. People have the potential to greatly increase our lives and to allow us to reach higher than we could in solitude. But people also have the potential to betray and take advantage of one another.

Another question we ought to ask is this: *Should we always forgive?*

FORGIVENESS

Let's begin with the definition of this sacred word. According to the *Merriam-Webster Dictionary*, to *forgive* means "*to cease to feel resentment against*" or to "*grant relief from a payment.*"[2]

Consider the second definition. If someone owes a debt, not canceling it is sometimes the right thing to do. For example, if someone borrows money, it is not right to always forgive the debt if they are capable of paying it. If debts were always forgiven, people would only take advantage of lenders and then lenders would stop lending money. But when we think of forgiveness, we are usually talking about the first definition—no longer feeling angry towards someone.

If someone hurts you, you can become bitter or angry with them, or you can forgive them. But if anger is appropriate under certain circumstances, then along the same vein, forgiveness is not always appropriate. Sometimes, it's good to build a wall to keep the perpetrator away.

By definition, forgiveness is "*to cease to feel resentment against.*" So if you have a proper reason to be angry, then you have a proper reason not to forgive.

There is a time for anger and for forgiveness, but this is not a time-sensitive matter, in the sense that there is no specific amount of time for forgiveness to be appropriate. You may feel less anger as the distance between you and the perpetrator widens, but you still ought to exercise caution before allowing that offender near you again.

We are often told to break down any walls we build between ourselves and those who have hurt us. But, logically speaking, should we forgive someone who has hurt us and will most likely hurt us again, or should we keep that wall up to protect ourselves? I would say it is best to keep it there. At least until they earn that trust back. And if they can never do that, do not remove the wall that protects you.

Cities have built walls for protection to keep their inhabitants safe. But walls always have a gate so that those inside can examine outside forces and use their judgment to either accept them or turn them away. How foolish would a nation be to forgive every nation they had fought or are currently fighting in a war and extend blind trust? Sometimes, you must protect yourself by opening the gates only after you believe the offender has repented and will not harm you again. Hence, the idea put forth in Ecclesiastes 3:5 supports this line of thought, saying, "*A time to embrace, and a time to refrain from embracing.*"

Resentment is a natural reaction that keeps us from continually falling for tricks played by malicious abusers. Despite its bad reputation, bitterness is valuable if used appropriately.

BITTERNESS

Some will say that not forgiving will lead to bitterness, and they are correct. Remembering how someone has harmed you usually leaves you with a bitter taste in your mouth, so you feel disgusted and turn away quickly.

Technically speaking, *bitterness* is a natural deterrent to stop us from eating something that is poisonous. If you eat food that is poisonous, your bitter taste receptors will let you know that you should no longer ingest that food. When we are bitter in response to things that we should not engage with, we should see bitterness as useful and something that allows us to thrive and live healthily.

Babies have a natural reaction to spit out any bitter-tasting food. The baby is unable to determine what is actually poisonous and what is acceptable to eat, and so he or she spits out anything that is bitter. As one grows older, one learns to determine what bitter foods are actually poisonous and those that are acceptable, but we should never lose the instinct to hate anything poisonous and harmful. As a child, strict rules of hating all bitter foods are acceptable because children are incapable of rationally deciding what is good for them. A man of high character should maintain the same instinct to avoid what is harmful and use rationality to determine how to best utilize this instinct.

I am not endorsing being bitter all the time and only possessing the virtue of bitterness. But when you are in contact with something that is poisonous and can hurt you, you should remember the previous experiences had with the entity. If it was truly poisonous and you have no reason to think it has changed, then you should have a bitter taste in your mouth so that you do not interact again. But when you are not in contact with something harmful, there is no need to have a bitter taste in your mouth.

Bitterness is also a virtue. A man of high character exhibits bitterness when he is disgusted at a person who is dangerous and poses a likely threat to the safety of innocent people.

FORGIVING WITHOUT FORGETTING

I am not saying that you should shut yourself out from the rest of the world; instead, take the optimal route. The lock on the door of a house is not always locked. If someone comes knocking, it can be opened when we feel safe or kept locked if we do not feel safe. It is best to be conscious and evaluate decisions individually instead of just taking one big ideology of locking the door and welding it shut or, contrarily, removing the door completely.

A wise man is conscious of his fears. He knows what may harm him, and he keeps an eye out for them. He bears his responsibilities such that he and those he is responsible for are safe. It may not always be bliss. It's responsibility and it's difficult, but it's also noble and worthwhile.

A man of high character forgives when he trusts. When a wrongdoer has truly repented, a man of high character forgives. He is not quick to assume that the other has changed, but he will not avoid the truth and hold a grudge when the other has indeed changed.

I did not always have this perspective on forgiveness. When I was young, I heard the following quote and tried to live by it:

"The stupid neither forgive nor forget;
The naïve forgive and forget;
The wise forgive but do not forget."

- Thomas Szasz[3]

As a child, I would not forget what had happened, but would forgive and not let it affect my life. Upon further consideration and with growing experience, I am more skeptical of the aforementioned phrase for I do not believe it is absolutely right. I do believe it is generally a good rule of thumb that children should follow, but an adult should have a more refined and developed understanding of when to display the virtue of forgiveness.

We must ask ourselves how we can separate forgiving from forgetting. It's extremely difficult, but that is not to say it can't or shouldn't be done. To forgive means that you no longer hold anything against the offender, but that would seem to go against the purpose of our memory. Surely our memory is retained to help us determine the best future path so that we do not repeat the same error over and over again. If you betray me and I continue to trust you and not hold your betrayal against you, would I not be a fool? It would be foolish to trust someone blindly after they betray you.

And if the wise remember the past but do not hold the past against someone, then wouldn't that neglect our need for memory? In fact, what would be the purpose of remembering an event at all if we are not going to use our memory to judge a future situation and be better prepared for the future?

Here is the solution: Forgiveness is wise when the future is not likely to resemble the past. In other words, if the transgressor has repented and you believe that they are for you and not against you, then they ought to be forgiven. Therefore, we retain the past betrayals in our memory but use the most useful and relevant memories, which include our memory of them repenting, for future decisions.

Never forget and forgive when you decide to trust.

Szasz's three lines are very close to being accurate. He is right that it is stupid to never forgive. If no one ever forgave, then there would be no trust and societies, families and friendships would fail. It is also naive to forgive and forget, for that is like starting fresh with no experience or wisdom. But those who are wise do not forgive under all circumstances. *The wise only forgive when they are fortunate.* Some have the good fortune of having people around them who ameliorate their shortcomings and earn their trust back. Only in that situation does a wise person forgive.

I must also say that we do have *some* control over the fortunes we encounter. If you tell your friend that they have hurt you, then they are made aware and have the ability to change themselves. But if you keep your bitterness to yourself, the bitterness will most likely remain. If you want to facilitate the rekindling of a relationship, you ought to give the other person a chance to know what they are doing is wrong. Some may call this *judging* and look at it negatively, but judging can actually be the greatest thing that you can do, for it allows you to keep your friends by giving them a chance to change their ways and earn back the trust that had been broken. The idea that God is called *The Ultimate Judge* who tells us what He believes is right and wrong is actually an honest gesture at friendship and welcoming. It all depends on perspective.

IGNORANT BLISS

To forgive means to no longer feel resentment or to no longer hold another accountable for something. However, if someone has repeatedly harmed you, you should remember that so you can properly protect yourself.

Yet, we are told to let go of all resentment and allow anger to vanish into thin air. That's radical for certain and I would even say incorrect. I believe the only time to forgive is under the following conditions:

1) Forgive when you are improperly or irrationally angry towards an individual or group that is undeserving of your anger; and

2) Forgive when the offender has repented, and you have decided to trust that the person will not harm you. If restitution is

owed, it must be paid unless mercy is granted.

Even as I write this, I am aware that many go through programs where they are taught to forgive, and, once they do, they feel a burden has been lifted off their shoulders. They feel bliss and happiness when the walls that have severed the relationship crumble. I have two thoughts about such a scenario.

1) Maybe that wall should never have been built, so a person would feel right about tearing it down. Since destroying the wall is the proper action to take, a person would be relieved when the burden disappears. Tearing down walls and restoring a relationship is truly a joyous moment.

2) Perhaps tearing down the wall was a mistake—ignorant bliss, so to speak. It's removing the consciousness of danger from your life when, in reality, it should still be in place.

Let me elaborate on the second point. I can walk through a jungle path and enjoy the beautiful sights, close my eyes, taking in the relaxing sounds of nature. I can do that without fear. It's so much less stressful when I don't allow fears or concerns to occupy my mind. However, enjoying the jungle to the point that I ignore the potential dangers is foolish.

The truth is that there are snakes and predators in the jungle. It is best to keep an eye open and watching for that which may seriously harm us. To ignore the realities of the jungle is to rid ourselves of all our fears and live in bliss.

We can decide to ignore the knowledge we have about the terrible things that can be done to us. We can decide that they don't concern us, and we can dance and sing and open the door to the world.

And then reality hits. A person with evil intentions walks in through that open door. Maybe we should have left it locked. Maybe that wall should have been left up. Was it worth the few moments of bliss?

Life is hard. Life has responsibilities. We can choose to ignore them, but we are no longer in Pleasureville where everything is perfect. We are in reality, and the best way to live in reality is to continually recall the knowledge of good and evil.

Forgiveness and fear are intertwined. If you believe you should fear, then you must believe that not everything ought to be forgiven. If you believe you should not have fears, then there is no reason to not forgive. Dr. Gerald Jampolsky, author of *Love Is Letting Go of Fear*, very much goes along with this thinking in his book:

> "*When we think we have been hurt by someone in the past, we build up defenses to protect ourselves from being hurt in the future. So, the fearful past causes a fearful future and the past and future become one. We cannot love when we feel fear... When we release the fearful past and forgive everyone, we will experience total love and oneness with all.*"[4]

His words are sweet but sadly misguided. He promotes ignorant bliss which is relieving but also dangerous. And the notion that love and fear cannot coexist is the most inaccurate statement one can make on the subject. Fear can only exist when you love. Love requires fear. Those who hate everything, including their own lives, walk around without fear or concern. Those who love their children are the ones who fear for their children's safety.

Just as a drug is easier to sell than the accomplishment of hard work, ignorant bliss is easier to sell than the truth.

Anger & War

To be unforgiving does not always require you to be in a state of anger. Unforgiveness can merely be a logical mindset of protecting yourself against something you no longer wish to encounter in the same manner as before. The unforgiving person may just be sad that they no longer are able to trust a friend. But, even if it does entail some anger, is that always wrong?

Obviously, if a perpetrator is not present in your life, you have no need to be angry at them. But if someone who robbed you in the past is busting down your door, anger is the proper response. Anger, like fear, builds up the *fight or flight* response. And haven't we learned that anger in the proper situation is the ideal state to be in?

We say vast blanket statements like "*violence is bad*," as if we have forgotten what the brave men in the Allied forces in the Second World War did. Surely, no one would say directly to them that stopping

Hitler's tyrannical conquest was wrong. Yet, some shout *"peace, not war"* as any battle wages. They blindly follow an ideology of peace without considering what is the right thing to do.

War is an expression of anger, merely more organized, calculated and on a grander scale. And anger toward the right person, to the right degree, at the right time, for the right purpose and in the right way is not only justified but also good.

To say that you should always forgive is to say that anger or being worried is always bad. What a foolish ideology! That is no different than to say that certain emotions or actions are categorically good or bad, and they most certainly are not.

All emotions have positive and negative aspects. Love can be overbearing; kindness can be deceitful; anger and rage can be useful; suffering can be meaningful; loyalty can be blinding; sadness can be revitalizing. To remove the ability to properly practice human characteristics would be to remove humanity. All emotions are good in the proper circumstances and bad when used at the incorrect time and place.

Most women do not even appreciate a man who is incapable of anger. This is why many like the *bad boy* archetype, to defend the woman and her children if needed. What better way to be defended than by someone who is enraged and is willing to fight to death? That anger will build up energy and adrenaline within you and allow the body to best handle the circumstances for a good and noble cause. That is virtuous! That ought to be respected! That's why women innately want a man with more muscles and athletic abilities; he is capable of danger and, therefore, capable of good.

A physically weak man is only capable of righteous acts when times are peaceful. Would you not rather have a man who is capable of righteousness at all times? A man of high character is one who can be brutish enough to fend off an attacker and yet wise enough to be kind in times of peace.

Yet, we teach men to submit to simple ideologies that are right in only some circumstances. We tell them to be weak so that they cannot harm us in times of peace. We tell them to always forgive, even when they should not. We are not aiming for righteousness. We do not preach becoming capable and great and using our capabilities at the proper time.

The Lie of Forgiving

Too often, we forgive someone who should not have been forgiven, and when we see the person again, all the bad memories and anger come rushing back. Our bodies have a natural reaction of repulsion to that which we do not trust. Naturally, our eyebrows scrunch up to scrutinize the situation because we are worried that person may hurt us again. We search for signs that they have changed to calm ourselves or we look for signs that they are going to do the same thing they did last time. If we have no legitimate reason to believe they have changed, we build up a wall again because this person is a potentially destructive force who seems to enjoy hurting others. We may have said that we forgave them, and we may have tried to make it appear sincere, but if we did it when we shouldn't have, then it may have just been a lie.

It may not have been a purposeful lie, but while forgiving, you may not have understood what is true forgiveness and when it should be granted. This is why it is so important that we understand forgiveness.

If you tell someone "*I forgive you*" and then blatantly show that you still hold them accountable for the hurt they had caused, then they will be mad at you for lying. For it is true that our actions speak louder than our words. And if our actions do not align with our words, then we are also betraying them.

We preach forgiveness, yet we do not follow it. We claim it, but we lie about it! We say that we forgive because it sounds sweet, but we still hold their actions against them! Those who receive such forgiveness are left betrayed and confused, for you say one thing and do another. You say that you hold nothing against them but then ask for the death penalty for their past mistakes. You say that you forgive them for cheating and then divorce them because they broke a promise. If we truly forgave the person, then we would treat them as if they did not do it. In other words, we would not hold it to their record after they are forgiven. That is forgiveness. That is how we expect others to forgive us. But we often do not forgive others in such a merciful way.

Those who say that they *forgive others in their hearts, but still hold them accountable* make the most foolish of arguments. Some simply say this to make themselves feel superior and noble, but in reality, they are liars. They say that they forgive the person for their sins but still hold them accountable. This is technically impossible. Imagine we get to heaven and God says, "*I forgave you in my heart, but I'm still sending you to hell because I need to hold you accountable for your sins.*" I think in that situation we would say that "*forgiving in your heart*" is not real forgiveness. Luckily, God does not do that; therefore, neither should we.

So do not lie! If you say you forgive them, absolve them completely! But if you have not done that yet, then do not lie and say that you have forgiven them!

I pray that you are able to forgive, but I pray more earnestly that you are given the opportunity to forgive and you only do so then.

RESTITUTION & REPENTANCE

Restitution is not always needed to show that you have repented, but when payment is owed, restitution is necessary. Restitution is, in a sense, a signal that you have repented for all your wrongdoings and are trying to undo the effects of the past mistake. To not pay restitution shows that you have not changed because you would rather hold on to the restitution owed more than you desire doing what is right.

Once a wrongdoing has been fully paid or mercy has been granted, only then should forgiveness be applied. In some circumstances, the debt cannot be repaid in full. Sometimes, the debt is more than the debtor has available or nothing could ever suffice to equal the payment. In such a case, mercy, which is the action of not delivering a punishment that is deserved, may be granted and forgiveness may be granted.

The American government projects this idea in their financial systems. For those who are unable to pay a debt, the government will allow for bankruptcy, but a person declaring bankruptcy must give up everything valuable they possess. Clearly, a financial institution would not be able to survive in the long run if people took advantage of such a system, so loans are only given to those who will be able to repay them or they make sure that you provide an equal sacrifice as collateral. If you do not have enough, then you need a co-signer who will bear the responsibility. It would be foolish for a large financial institution to trust everyone and to forgive as soon as someone asks for it.

After the sin has been paid for, the sinner must also repent. In Luke 17, Jesus tells his followers, *"Pay attention to yourselves! If your brother sins, rebuke him, and if he repents, forgive him."* It is only after the brother repents that you forgive.

In Matthew 18, Jesus tells his followers, *"If your brother sins against you, go and tell him his fault, between you and him alone. If he listens to you, you have gained your brother. But if he does not listen, take one or two others along with you, that every charge may be established by the evidence of two or three witnesses. If he refuses to listen to them, tell it to the church. And if he refuses to listen even to the church, let him be to you as a Gentile and a tax collector."* Jesus does not instruct us to forgive one another right away and without regard for the circumstances. He teaches us to forgive only when someone repents and changes their ways; otherwise, we are to treat them differently.

Some people think that the Bible preaches forgiveness to everyone, but that doesn't seem to be realistic and businesses that do so will not succeed. Where is the disconnect? We have been indoctrinated with the idea that *to forgive is divine*, and Bible verses are often stated out of context that make people lean toward unconditional forgiveness:

> *"Be kind to one another, tenderhearted, forgiving one another, as God in Christ forgave you."*
> - Ephesians 4:32

From a quick reading of the aforementioned verse, you may think that the Bible supports the idea that it is always best to forgive. What we must keep in mind is who the author, Paul, is speaking to. He is writing to fellow believers of Christ, who are at the church of Ephesus. The main theme of the letter to the church, as stated by New

Testament scholar Daniel Wallace, is *"Christians, get along with each other!"* He states that the purpose of the letter is *"intended on getting Christians to grow in unity and love with one another."*[5]

When verses do promote *always forgiving*, we must look at the context—it is only referring to forgiving those who are also committed to pursuing righteousness, which is the calling of those who follow Christ's teachings; therefore, you should assume that they will not pursue your detriment if you assume they are aiming for righteousness. And if you are being righteous by forgiving those who are your brothers (aiming at righteousness), then God will know that you are aiming at righteousness and you will be forgiven. But if you do not do what is right and withhold forgiveness from someone who deserves it, then you should not be forgiven for you are not pursuing righteousness.

We must take the instructions given to the church of Ephesus in the context that they should only be applied within the church. For example, the previous verse in Ephesians 4 states that we should *"Let all bitterness and wrath and anger and clamor and slander be put away from you, along with all malice."* Many Christians think that we should stay away from bitterness, anger and wrath as if Ephesians 4:31 concluded that such things are absolutely immoral in all circumstances. But the truth is that this verse only relates to the way a Christian ought to feel towards another Christian. Otherwise, wouldn't we have to conclude that Jesus was sinning when he was angry in the temple and that God's wrath is sinful? And aren't we to emulate God? Yet, too often we hear that we should never be angry or bitter as if these characteristics were absolute evils.

Forgive as God has forgiven you. This idea is found in Ephesians 4:32 and repeated in Colossians 3:13. Many believe it means to forgive unconditionally, but what they often forget is that God's forgiveness is very much conditional. God hasn't been dishing out forgiveness for every sin ever committed.

The next verse given to the church of Ephesus is *"Therefore be imitators of God, as beloved children."* Do as God does.

Perhaps you think I am wrong about the concept of forgiveness.

You may say that I am misunderstanding the verses and their context and that we should forgive everyone. But if I am wrong, then wouldn't that contradict how God forgives? God denies heaven to most people because they are not forgiven for the sins they committed against God. They are sent to hell. Therefore, God does not unconditionally forgive all people. And if we are to forgive as God does, then how do you reconcile the two beliefs? You must either admit that the Bible contradicts itself or forgive as God forgives. Remember, the only time God offers unconditional forgiveness is when someone agrees to the covenant that is offered. Just like in marriage.

GOD'S REQUIREMENTS

In 1709, Alexander Pope wrote the often-quoted line, "*To err is human, to forgive, divine.*"[6] But is forgiveness inherently divine? No. It is divine to be capable of forgiveness and then choosing to forgive only when the person has repented and paid for their sin.

Two things are required from you in order for you to receive forgiveness from God—*repentance* and *acceptable sacrifice.*

According to the Bible, the cost of sin is death (Romans 6:23). So God sent down his own son, Jesus, to pay for the sins you committed. He was perfect, sinless, spotless; therefore, he was able to pay for your sins when you could not. God would not forgive your sins without restitution being paid.

Prior to Jesus's sacrifice, Jews would sacrifice animals at the altar to pay for their sins. The idea was that they would take the best sacrificial animal they had, one that had no blemishes and was spotless, and they would slaughter it. The animal had to be spotless because the repentance needed to be the best you could offer. As the animal itself was not even enough to pay for your sins, the least you could do was offer the best you had.

Currently, Jews do not sacrifice animals and have not been sacrificing animals since 70 AD.[7] They stopped because the Torah (the first five books of the Old Testament) required all animal sacrifices to be made at the Temple in Jerusalem, which has been destroyed. When the Jews rebuild the Temple in Jerusalem, where a mosque currently stands, then the sacrifices will continue.

Imagine if animal sacrifices were still carried out today. Imagine knowing that your sins would result in the death of an animal. We might actually repent and really stop sinning, knowing that a certain sheep would be killed for a sin we consider committing. It puts a direct tangible cost on our sins and we ought to feel guilty for our shortcomings. That's why animals were used as a sacrifice. That's why repentance is so important. Repentance changes the future.

Now that Jesus has died for our sins, the acceptable sacrifice has been made; however, we didn't make the sacrifice. So, have we repented? The Bible says that whoever believes in Jesus is granted salvation. Salvation, which leads to being forgiven and allowed into heaven, is only given to those who follow Jesus's teachings. Many believe you just have to believe that Jesus existed because they have always heard "*believe in him.*" But belief in His existence is different from believing in His teachings. For even in the Bible, demons and unbelievers met and knew Jesus but were not going to attain salvation.

In order to show repentance, the path that Jesus taught needs to be followed. To be on the path is to show that you are no longer embracing the sinful life but trying to run away from it and towards Jesus's teachings. In other words, if you follow Jesus's teachings, then you are trying to follow only what is good; you are now committed to righteousness and, therefore, trying to turn away from everything that is bad. What is repentance other than turning from the bad toward the good? Therefore, when you turn to Jesus's teachings and commit to them, you are repenting for all your sins. Therefore, Jesus *paid for all sins* with His death and you *repented for all bad things* by following Jesus, and the end result is that you are granted *forgiveness for all of your sins.*

Since repentance is separate from restitution, only a God who knows our unspoken thoughts can know if we have repented by truly devoting ourselves to Jesus's teachings.

HOW TO KNOW IF YOU SHOULD FORGIVE

First, we will address the idea of restitution. To put it simply, it is up to you. You have the ability to hold someone accountable for what they owe you or you can grant them mercy and forgive their debt. Just know that if you do grant mercy, never come back and demand the payment later.

But how are you to know if someone has repented? God can know everyone's thoughts, but people are not capable of reading minds. So, we must use our own abilities to determine if a person has repented. Trust can be earned back over time by an offender continually doing what is right. A sincere apology with the acknowledgment of the sin may convince some. Remorse and attempting to remedy the problem are even better. But none of these are guaranteed to prove repentance, for we know not what the person asking for forgiveness is truly thinking. A person who enjoys taking advantage of others will do anything necessary to regain trust in themselves, just to be able to take advantage again.

When those in the public domain, people of power, are caught in a scandal, they may lie to regain the trust of their supporters. It seems that every time a celebrity does something wrong, they immediately donate a sum of money to a cause to make themselves seem like a person who actually cares about others. This could be done out of honesty or because their manager wants to buy back your trust.

It is up to you to determine if you should forgive someone. Use your best judgment and conscience to determine if they have repented. But once you do believe they have repented, forgive them.

PERSONAL FORGIVENESS

If you are not convinced that they have truly changed, then do not forgive them. On the other hand, if you believe that they have repented, then let it go.

For example, in early 2019, Virginia's Governor and Attorney General, both Democrats, had admitted to wearing blackface in the 1980s. Voters supporting both political parties called for their resignation and would not forgive them. The two men apologized and publicly denounced their actions in the past. In fact, if you look at their record in office prior to the discovery, they had been doing what they thought was best to help the African American community and were extremely respectful to them during their entire time in office. You could almost say that these men catered to the African American community and have obviously changed their path and currently are not the kind of people who would even consider mocking or disrespecting African Americans. Yet, they are not forgiven. Obviously, this is not a judicial matter, and they should not be penalized by the courts, but it is a matter of personal forgiveness. Should the voters hold their actions from the 1980s against them? Or should they forgive them as they have obviously repented? I would say that they ought to be forgiven and that what they did decades ago is no longer relevant to what they currently believe.

Another example to discuss would be Larry Nassar. Nassar was the doctor of the USA national gymnastics team who admitted to molesting multiple children and athletes whom he oversaw. At least 250 females have come forward with accusations of his criminal acts. Hypothetically, let's say that Larry has served time and wants to practice as a physician again in the future. First, I would find it nearly impossible to believe that he has truly repented and is not faking his new lifestyle so that he can get back into his old position. It is possible that he may have changed, but I would not be easily convinced that he is truly changed.

If you cannot trust Larry Nassar to be your doctor again, or the doctor of your child, then I would not recommend that you say that you have forgiven him because you are still holding him accountable for his past wrongdoings. Nassar has done things that have earned him some trust, such as taking the Hippocratic Oath, but he has also done some things that have destroyed any trust toward him, such as molesting his patients. If you are saying that you will forgive him for what he has done, then you should go back to treating him like any other doctor who has some level of trust. I personally don't think you should forgive him or trust him.

THE FORGIVING AND UNFORGIVING MIND

Our memory is given to us so that we can remember the past and be better prepared for the future. Often, the past does repeat itself. Fear is useful in ensuring our future is different from our past if our past was harmful. We are only born with two fears—loud noises and falling. We gain other fears after we experience or learn about things that may harm us so that we are not harmed by them in the future. Only an idiot who does not fear would continually walk into a dangerous situation and expect good things to happen. And if he does not learn from the danger and has no fear the next day, he will repeat the past and continually do what is foolish and insane.

To encounter something that we fear will result in the *fight or flight* reaction. *Flight* can be the exact opposite of wanting conflict, but if you have no fear, then you will surely walk into the situation and face whatever conflict might arise.

This lifestyle of following certain virtues whole-heartedly and without any consideration of what is right is a childish ideology. We are like babies, without rationality, wanting a simplistic, unconditional rule to follow. Shouldn't we aim to be greater than that?

We have tried to convince ourselves that unconditional forgiveness is the right thing to do because it feels good in the short term. It's a drug we can't stop consuming. But one day, it will all come crashing down. You will get to the point where the drug needs to be tripled because a double dose has no impact on your happiness. As we drink down more lies, we will get to the point where we either overdose or bear the misery of withdrawal when we have confronted the undeniable truth that unconditional forgiveness is not the right ideology to embrace.

The truth is that we should be afraid of some snakes. The venomous ones that harm us do not change their ways. So, we hold that potential harm against their character and are afraid when they are near. We build a wall to protect ourselves from those snakes. It is the *fight or flight* mechanism that keeps us safe when we encounter them because we know their capabilities. But if venomous snakes stopped biting or if they learned to talk and tell us that they would stop biting, then they could earn our trust back. We could tear down that wall that keeps us safe from them. We would no longer need the *flight or fight* response. Such relief! It would be bliss to walk through a jungle and not have to worry about a snake bite! But sadly, that is not reality. Snakes that bite are still a threat, and we need proper mechanisms to keep ourselves safe from them because nothing has changed, and they will hurt you.

I am not saying never forgive. On the contrary, I am telling you to forgive properly and rationally. If you were to unconditionally forgive and then be hurt over and over again because the person never truly repented, you will most likely get to a point where you consider forgiveness as a pretty bad idea. For that would be the rational point to come to. That does not mean you should not forgive; it just means that you should learn to forgive properly. Do it in a way that was given as an example for us.

Proper forgiveness will not always make you feel happy and relieved in the short term because it might require facing the reality that you ought not to forgive. However, only forgiving when someone deserves it will significantly reduce the chances of you being attacked by monsters when they have not repented and will keep you from burning out on the childish idea of unconditional forgiveness. It is a long-term strategy to keep you guarded, which allows you to continually forgive when you ought to.

FORGIVING YOURSELF

Dare I say the truth that you should not always forgive yourself? Yes! For it is good to aim to be in a place where you should forgive yourself, but until you are in such a place, you should not.

Therefore, commit to the betterment of yourself. If you have evil or childish ways that caused you hurt, then repent and change paths. Aim to better yourself so you can forgive yourself. Perhaps being bitter at ourselves is the proper mindset we should be in until we change paths and manifest a proper aim. It is only natural to live a life where we love ourselves if we have a proper aim.

You should not forgive yourself unless you can trust that you are working toward self-betterment! How beautiful an idea is that! *To resolve the bitterness of our own existence, the only thing we can do is work to better ourselves.* As we see that we are truly aiming to better ourselves, then we will trust ourselves and then we will forgive ourselves of our shortcomings.

To try to forgive yourself while you do not work on bettering yourself is a lie that your own subconscious will reject. You cannot alleviate the bitterness you experience towards yourself if you are continually harming yourself. Only working towards good will allow you to not resent your own self.

We naturally have a bitterness towards ourselves when we do not trust ourselves completely. If we engage with poisonous objects or if we continually put ourselves in bad positions, we ought to hate that part of our selves. Therefore, refrain from that which you cannot handle properly. When you are able to handle something without it causing more harm than good, then engage with it if it is worthwhile.

"And if your right hand causes you to sin, cut it off and throw
it away. For it is better that you lose one of your members than
that your whole body go into hell."
- Matthew 5:30

Obviously you don't have to literally cut off your hand, but consider the idea that if you can't handle something that is poisoning yourself then you should separate yourself from it. Throw away your phone. Stay away from places you should not visit. Only when you are capable of handling something properly should you engage with it. When you are not being so destructive toward your own self and choose to let yourself grow, then you will love yourself.

Some will say that holding on to resentment and bitterness will hurt you more than it hurts the person you are bitter towards; sometimes, this is true. However, sometimes, bitterness protects you more than it costs to bear such bitterness.

"The proverb warns that 'You should not bite the hand that
feeds you.' But maybe you should if it prevents you from feeding
yourself."
- Thomas Szasz[8]

In addition to the idea of how to properly engage with the virtue of forgiveness, we can also learn how to properly ask for forgiveness from others. When you sin or do not act properly, in order to obtain proper forgiveness, you must do your best to repay any debt and repent. Do not shrug off your errors and ignore them. Take responsibility for them and allow them to transform you into the person who will try not to commit the same error again in the future. This will be your best chance at regaining another's trust, and even then, it may not be enough because they cannot truly know that you have repented. You must understand that a rational person might still be skeptical, but you can put yourself in the best circumstance going forward when you are seeking forgiveness.

Unconditional forgiveness is only to be given to those who are truly aimed at your betterment. So make a commitment to live righteously, so that you can forgive yourself. Forgive your wife, because she has committed to your betterment. But do not forgive your enemies who seek to kill you.

So, what are we to learn from this? Be trustworthy and repent of your wrongdoings. Doing so allows people to forgive you. Trustworthiness is admired because it brings people closer together and allows them to forgive and continue a friendship that is beneficial to both parties.

THE PAST

History often repeats itself. You do to. But the cycle can be broken. Repentance can occur. You can look at your own life and determine if this is what you want—if this is the kind of person you want to be. You can repent for your sins and repair your insufficiencies and realize you want to be better and actually pursue what is good and virtuous. It will not come without looking introspectively and trying to understand what needs to be altered. You will be judged on your past when people project your future, but make sure that there is a part of your past that has had a revolution and has changed your misguided direction and that you are now aiming at righteousness.

"There can be only one permanent revolution — a moral one;
the regeneration of the inner man.
How is this revolution to take place? Nobody knows how it will
take place in humanity, but every man feels it clearly in himself.
And yet in our world everybody thinks of changing humanity,
and nobody thinks of changing himself."
- Leo Tolstoy[9]

CHAPTER 3

"Keep your eyes wide open before marriage,
half shut afterwards."
- Benjamin Franklin[1]

The Death of Marriage

Trust & Faith

Is marriage an institution that fails to keep up with the times? Will the institution of marriage survive another generation? Or will it slowly fade away like an old institution that was only ideal for past generations? Has marriage died the same death that Friedrich Nietzsche was referring to when he declared that *"God is dead"*[2]?

Most cultures tell us to move in the direction of marriage, and we often do so because someone we care about encourages it or we want our kids to grow up in a family with married parents. While those reasons are valid and ought to be considered, we cannot neglect the true essence of marriage and what we should be looking for in a life partner. We often tell the young to marry their *best friend*. However, we should tell them to marry someone that they have deep passionate and instinctual love for and have rationally decided that the other person is compatible and trustworthy.

Yet, we tell others to marry their best friend. Imagine if you were meeting an old friend and he introduced you to his wife by saying, *"Hey, I want to introduce you to my friend, Janice."* You can imagine the disapproving glare his wife would give him for not choosing the best possible title he could bestow upon her. Even *girlfriend* or *fiancée* means so much more than *friend* or *best friend*. Marriage is not just permanently establishing a best friend. It is in a whole other category of relationships. We regress when we put marriage in the same category as all other relationships. Marriage is the only relationship in which all wrongs are forgiven without condition, for it is the only relationship that contains a vow to always trust each other. I sincerely hope you marry someone who is your best friend and whom you get along with. I hope you delight in each other's company. But I also hope that they are more than just your *best friend*. If your marriage is built on the foundation of happiness and how much you like someone, then it will crumble when the marriage inevitably faces hard times. However, if your marriage is founded on something sturdier, something that does not change over time, then it may survive though the lows and flourish in the highs.

TRUST

Should you trust? That is too vague a question.

Should you trust your spouse? Most say "*Yes!*" but when they are actually tested, they find that they do not believe it deep down—it is still too vague a question.

Should you trust your spouse if you suspect them of cheating on you? Because if you investigate, then you are not trusting. What if someone gives you reasonable evidence of infidelity? Would you continue to blindly trust them?

This is an interesting scenario to ponder. In reality, people do not unconditionally trust their spouses but like to cling to the idea that trust within a marriage should be boundless and unconditional. I believe that trust must remain within bounds and should not be applied to everything.

For example, should you trust that your wife knows the answer to an advanced calculus question? No, you shouldn't trust that she will know the answer unless she is a qualified mathematician. Should you trust that your wife will work for your betterment and that of the relationship? Yes, because that was promised in the marriage vows. Unconditional trust, or better yet *faith*, that your spouse will *aim for your betterment and that of the relationship* is what distinguishes marriage from friendships.

We say that we should trust our spouse, but most of us have no idea what that actually means and within what boundaries. But we have to know! We must understand what we are signing up for; otherwise, marriage is just another meaningless act. The problem we face is not that we trust but that we trust in the wrong areas and lack trust in the right areas.

Some say that we should have absolute trust in God and our spouse. There are situations in which they get mad at God, for instance, when He does nothing to allow a child to live through cancer, especially when they trusted God would answer their prayers. But they forget that God never promised good health.

God never promised any of us a mansion. So, why would you trust that He would give it to you? You would not walk up to a stranger and say, "*I trust that you will give me $5,*" and become disappointed when it is not given.

God did promise salvation if you properly seek forgiveness—and that you can trust. There are certain things that you can rely on God to do, but trusting that He will give you a mansion and all of the riches of the world is only going to lead to disappointment.

The same goes for a spouse. We get mad when they do not fulfill our expectations that were not made in the marriage vows, and then we say that they have broken all of our trust.

We no longer know how to go about trusting. We make everything black and white. We say that if we cannot always trust someone in all respects, then we will have zero trust. We have made it all or nothing, but marriage was not designed for complete trust in a person for everything. Those who expect complete unconditional trust must either blind themselves to reality or give up on any trust in marriage. It is only unconditional trust that your spouse will *aim for your betterment and that of the relationship.* But most do not bother to define the limits of their unconditional trust.

Therefore, many have decided to ignore trust completely. We have replaced it with a new philosophy: we are marrying our *best friend.*

A best friend is usually trustworthy, but a best friend does not have the same type of trust present in a covenant. We have downgraded marriage in order to keep the tradition alive, but we do not act as if we are married anymore. We must not throw out the entire concept of trust from marriage but instead learn the proper times for trusting and not trusting.

To understand how marriages work, we will have to actually understand the proper way to treat a spouse in comparison to how a friend should be treated.

EARNINGS (JUSTICE) AND GIFTS (MERCY AND GRACE)

Let us take a step back and understand how any relationship works. When we interact with someone who has made a mistake, we can either pursue justice or we can act with mercy and grace.

Those who pursue justice love being rewarded and will allow punishments to persist because they believe that people ought to be accountable and rewarded for the talent, effort, skills and decision that make them who they are.

Those who pursue mercy and grace love equity (to some degree) and think everyone deserves an equal outcome, regardless of the effort or skills they display. They care more about making sure everyone is feeling happy and not left out, despite the fact that some deserve less and some deserve more. They believe that everyone should receive an equal piece of the pie or at least some of the pie and that those who are more fortunate ought to be gracious with the less fortunate. When you show unconditional mercy, responsibilities are irrelevant because everything is forgiven, and successes are shared amongst others.

For every increase in mercy or grace, you sacrifice justice. Likewise, for every increase in justice, you sacrifice mercy or grace. To illustrate this point, consider what is the point of learning and becoming more knowledgeable if it doesn't matter and the end result is the same for everyone? You would surely want the suffering you persisted through in order to learn and obtain capabilities to be worthwhile. And if all the end results are the same, then your increase in knowledge is wasteful and provides no value. What motivation do you have to go through learning how to become skilled, if the amount of skill you have makes no difference in your salary or life?

To have a world that is perfectly just, where punishments are carried out for every wrongdoing, means that we have no mercy or grace toward others. We will see people repent and change and become citizens that will further our society, and still keep them locked away for a mistake they made before they changed. We sacrifice the ideal and the maximizing of value. On the contrary, to have a world that is perfectly gracious and merciful would deprive people of the desire to improve their lives.

No one's mindset is completely justice or mercy/grace oriented, as we often possess a percentage of each of these two characteristics that add up to 100%. When previously discussing how to properly forgive, I emphasized using justice and only using mercy when the person repents. When we interact with most people, having a predominantly judgmental (justice) approach is ideal.

Having a judgmental mindset will allow you to value someone's character. You compile all the rights and wrongs you hold to a person's account, and then you determine if you would like to be their friend or acquaintance. *You can add up all the facts about a person before determining if you trust them.* We use logic to determine if we believe they will benefit or hurt us. When looking for a spouse, nothing could be more important and should be the main priority while dating. You should judge them and determine if they would be a suitable and trustworthy partner.

A RECORD OF RIGHTS AND WRONGS

Should we retain a record of the wrongs of another person? A friend of mine told me that I should be able to judge someone's character without having to keep a record of wrongs because "*love keeps no record of wrongs*"[3] according to 1 Corinthians 13:5. Therefore, if we are to *love everyone*, then we must not keep a record of wrongs and judge others. This idea did not sit too well with me.

My response was that the only way to judge or know the trustworthiness of a person is to keep a record of rights and wrongs, and therefore, I will continue to do so. However, I must mention, and will later explain that the only exception to this is marriage.

The reason I believe it is proper to *hold a record of wrongs* is that the only way we can test the character of someone is based on their actions. We then compile all of their actions and choices and determine their character. There is no other way of determining someone's character.

For example, imagine you know someone who lies to you consistently. You should choose not to involve yourself with this person because you find their character to be immature or deceitful. But if the person stops acting in such a manner and begins making the right decisions, then your judgment of the person's character would change and you might befriend them.

I believe this way of thinking, which I have defined as *justice*, is proper for judging anyone who is not your spouse. Consider another example: if you were close friends with someone and they consistently lied to you, wouldn't your motivation to talk to such a person diminish? Or if your friend did a horrendous crime, should you not count that wrong against their character? Wouldn't you recommend that I spend less or no time with such a person who has committed heinous crimes? If you would recommend that, then you are recommending that I keep a record of wrongs.

That being said, we must understand what it is meant by the idea that *love keeps no record of wrongs*. There are two main words that we need to consider in the phrase—*love* and *record*. To begin with the latter, when the verse says, "*keeps no record*," the Greek word that is used is *logizetai*[4], which is derived from *logos* meaning *logic*. Knowing the definition, the verse says that love does not include logic, reasoning, accounting or thinking. Now, let us look at the former part of the phrase, which in Greek is *agapē* and which we have interpreted as *love*. As there are many different types of love, we must consider what this type of love applies to.

It is not friendly or brotherly love because the Greek word would have been *philia* (hence, Philadelphia is called the City of Brotherly Love). It is not the love that is a sexual passion, for then the Greek word would have been *erōs* (hence, the modern word erotic). It is not a practical and convenient type of love, for then the Greek word *pragma* could have sufficed (hence, pragmatic relationships). The word used is *agapē*, from which we derive very few, if any, words from in English. It is said to be the love used to describe God's love for people and the way people should love God.

So, the question remains—what is the *agapē* that God has for man? Answer: The unconditional mindset of desiring a proper relationship with another, one where it is always possible to reconcile and become close. It is the idea that regardless of what you do, there is always a desire and means to rekindle a friendship and make it right. It is the mindset that we should have for humanity, that no matter what evil things happen, we should be delighted when someone turns from evil ways and pursues goodness so that you can now have a proper relationship. *Agapē* is the desire to have a relationship with someone and doing so only *if you trust them*. This is why we are to *agapē* our enemies but still bring them to justice if they are not meeting the standards of civility that we expect from them.

In the same way, you can have *agapē* for your neighbor, hate some humans who do terrible things and affectionately love those who are trustworthy friends. This is why God can have *agapē* for everyone, "*hate all evildoers*" (Psalm 5:5) and have an affectionate love towards those who love Him (John 16:27).

Whenever God's *agapē* is described, it is shown to be a mindset that he has towards people. It is a mindset that desires a relationship, but requires trust before a relationship is established.

How can we say that God loves everyone, all the while defining love in such a way that contradicts the actions of God? Do you blind yourself to the reality that God does build up a record of wrongs and His patience runs out with some people? The only reasonable answer that one can hold, while remaining a Christian, is that this word *agapē* is not referring to actions, but a mindset. Despite this, we continue to preach that we should devote ourselves to unconditionally practicing specific actions when interacting with our neighbors and our enemies.

Agapē is a mindset that never changes. It is a mindset that is perfectly patient and does not change regardless of the wrongs someone does. No wrong can remove the mindset that God has for you (hence, it is unaffected by knowledge or logic). At any point, if you turn to him, he will accept you. It is a mindset that does not insist on its own ways but rejoices when you turn from evil so that now you can be accepted. That is perfect *agapē*.

> *"You have heard that it was said, 'You shall agapē your*
> *neighbor and hate your enemy.' But I say to you, agapē your*
> *enemies and pray for those who persecute you."*
> - Matthew 5:43–44[5]

The Greek term *agapē* was used by the apostles in the New Testament because they wanted to describe this unique idea that was unlike anything they had ever experienced. The apostles took a word that was unestablished in Greek and decided to use it to express the teaching of Jesus. This is why 1 Corinthians 13 takes the time to define *agapē* by describing the word so that people could understand it.

Why did they use a word that had no established definition? Answer: Because *agapē* was a new concept that Jesus was introducing— it was a concept that teaches righteousness and not the blind following of a certain virtue. Yet, we still translate *agapē* as love despite the fact that the apostles chose not to use any of the available forms of love.

Love is either a feeling (brought about by natural reactions) or an action you choose to do. *Agapē* is a mindset. To be blunt—*agapē* should not be translated as *love*.

To say that our actions or our feelings should not be affected by what others do is nonsense. To say that our mindset should not be affected by what others do makes sense. In a game of chess, we should base our actions off of what others do, but we should always have a mindset focused on victory regardless of their moves.

We should always have a mindset to pursue proper relationships— that is *agapē*. It should be consistent and unconditional for all people. Practically, this means that you may have to deny a relationship with some if they do not meet your standards and, therefore, do not trust them. *Agapē* is unconditional, but love (brotherly, romantic, pragmatic, etc.) is conditional.

When John 15:13 says that *"Greater love has no one than this, that someone lay down his life for his friends,"* we see that *agapē* results in the willingness to suffer for friends or those who are close with the person.

It does not include suffering for those who are our enemies. Yes, we should have unconditional *agapē* for all, but that *agapē* results in only having love for those whom we trust.

When John 3:16 says that "*God so loved the world that he gave his only begotten son*," the word love is the Greek *agapē*. It is used because God so deeply wanted to have a relationship with people that He sent His own son down to die in order to create a path of reconciliation for our sins so that we could have a relationship with Him. God did not reconcile with everyone automatically, but only those who chose to turn away from their evil ways. I cannot stress this point enough—*agapē* does not mean solving problems and forcing a relationship but desiring a relationship to happen and only then having a relationship if the other person is willing to put in the work to have a proper relationship.

The reason *agapē* contains no logic or reasoning is because *agapē* wants a relationship regardless of another's shortcomings. It doesn't mean that you ignore the problems that need to be reconciled but that you have a desire to have a proper relationship with another. In other words, it is a desire to have a relationship with someone, and doing so when they have earned your trust. It promotes the idea of a community because you are not permanently shunning one person or a group of people but are creating a path to friendship and reconciliation when it is broken. Do not shut out others when they meet your standards by being for you and not against you; embrace those who are worthy of your friendship. It is a rational and virtuous way of going about fellowship and allowing a community to become a properly functioning society

God has *agapē* for us, which does not move when we make mistakes. *The desire to have a relationship with us is always there no matter what we do.* There is no wrong that can undo *agapē*.

God does judge whether or not we are worthy of His friendship and fellowship, as we can see by His title of being the Ultimate Judge of people and His keeping of a record of rights and wrongs. Sins that have been committed are what prevent people from entering heaven and those sins are kept on *record* until they are forgiven.

Agapē is not an equal treatment. It is an equal consideration.

So, should we too have this *agapē* for our neighbor and everyone? Yes. Should we keep a record of the rights and wrongs of everyone? Yes (with the exception of marriage). It just means that regardless of the wrongs, we should continue to desire a relationship with someone and doing so if they earn our trust back. When the Bible says to *love thy neighbor*, it does not mean to have a relationship or friendship with everyone, otherwise the word would have been *philia*. No! Your neighbor could be a terrible person. It uses the word *agapē* because it means that you are willing to have fellowship with them if they meet your standards and that, no matter what wrongdoings are committed, you should always be willing to have that relationship when they do change and earn your trust.

I do believe that the current translation of 1 John 4:19 is wrong. I do not think that "*We love because [God] first loved us.*" I believe that we were shown a mindset of desiring a proper relationship with everyone because we were able to see God do this first. We were able to see God forgive His enemies when they repented, and we should emulate this mindset. But do we actually love because God first loved us? No. God actually hates many people that do not love Him. In fact, the only time God is shown to have an affectionate love is in John 16:27 where God has a brotherly love towards believers *because they loved Him*. I believe that God only loves those who first love Him. However, we have this beautiful idea of *agapē* because God first showed us *agapē*.

It is not customary for people to fully forgive his enemies in the sense that *agapē* demands of us. Often, one will hold his neighbors in higher regard than others who he once was against, even if they are both equally good now. As Nietzsche said, "*When we have to change our mind about a person, we hold the inconvenience he causes us very much against him.*"[6] But this concept of *agapē* teaches us to not hold ones past against them if they do change. Value them for their expected future value, do not let it be muddled by the past that they have changed from. It is a more righteous way of judging.

MARRIAGE

Let's summarize the main points thus far:

1) A normal relationship should consist of logical judgment (justice) to determine if a person has earned your trust.
2) If someone is trustworthy, then be their friend.
3) In a marriage, you are trusting that your spouse will work for the betterment of you and your relationship because that is what is implied or stated in the vows.

In the Bible, a Christian choosing to follow God is compared to a bride being married to her groom. This idea should be the foundation for marriage. Once a Christian is saved, God trusts that you are truly devoted to Him and are aiming at honoring His teachings. You may screw up, but God believes that you are still aiming at doing what is right for that is what a Christian vows to do. Therefore, God, who is omniscient, trusts you and always forgives those who are devoted to Him.

Never forget and forgive when you decide to trust.

Only after a Christian is saved and committed to God, does God not keep a record of wrongs. Until then, your wrongs are on record.

Likewise, only after a man is married should he not keep a record of the wrongs of his wife. To be married to someone is to say that you will trust them regardless of what they do because you know that they are committed to loving you.

Therefore, since you trust them in that regard, then you are saying that you will no longer keep a record of their wrongs. You will always forgive.

Never forget and forgive when you decide to trust.

You are giving up *justice* and now only using 100% of the *mercy and grace* aspects. If they begin to lie to you or do not treat you as an ideal friend, you may not leave them because you two are tied together. You should not chip away points from their friendship score. You can only forgive, and no longer think of them as less as you might towards a friend.

Never forget and forgive when you decide to trust.

God's standard is perfection. Only those who are perfect will get into heaven. Imagine if God said to you, *"I know we have this covenant, but I'm going to judge you for one or two really bad things you have done that I do not want to let go of."* Then, you are definitely destined for hell. In the same way, if you judge your spouse at all and hold some things against your spouse, then you do not understand what marriage is.

"Do not judge, or you too will be judged. For in the same way you judge others, you will be judged, and with the measure you use, it will be measured to you."

- Matthew 7:1–2

This verse clearly does not apply to all types of judging outside of marriage. You judge houses when you look to buy one. You judge the women you are interested in when dating. You judge friends to see who is compatible with you. We all judge, and we should be judged. Jesus says only moments after the aforementioned verse that you should watch out for false prophets and not throw your pearls to pigs. In other words, judge the character of someone to determine if you should interact with them.

There is nothing wrong with judging. There is only error in prejudice, which is pre-judging or judging something before you have enough information to make a proper judgement.

But when you enter into a covenant, then you should not judge your spouse because you are trusting in the promises that the two of you have made to each other. If you do judge and hold something against your spouse, then you too deserve judgment because you are not holding up your end of the deal. Therefore, why should God honor a covenant with you if you break the covenant you have with your spouse?

COVENANT AND CONTRACT

A covenant is a promise to do something regardless of what the other party does. The New Covenant promises that God will forgive anyone who follows Jesus's teachings. There is nothing you can do to take away this promise. A contract, on the other hand, is an agreement that can be canceled when one person fails to meet expectations. What is marriage? You can often tell if something is a contract if there are ways to break the contract and no longer receive the promised deal. If divorce is possible, then marriage is simply not a covenant.

So, does this mean marriage is merely a contract? No. It is a combination of the two. Marriage is a covenant whose limits are set by the vows taken by the pair. It has the love of a covenant because you are to fully love the other person regardless of what they do, with the exception of breaking the vows. Until the vows are broken, you are to love the person regardless of the fact that you think that they are not holding up their end sufficiently. This does not mean you tolerate their abuse and harm, for even Jesus said to separate yourself from a part of your own body if it is against yourself.

While your spouse may fall short in their goal at times, they should always have *the aim* of working for your betterment. They should never blaspheme or hope to destroy you for that proves that you are no longer committed to aiming for their betterment.

BITTERNESS

My friend who originally proposed the idea that we should not *keep a record of wrongs* based the idea on the premise that doing so will lead to bitterness. And the truth is, my friend was right. To keep a record of wrongs will lead to bitterness. But my friend forgot one essential aspect: we have the ability to forgive others when they repent. If we do not forgive others, we will be led down a path that contains much bitterness. Knowing this, I would say that we ought to repent so that others do not become bitter towards us.

For example, if you punch a random person, they will be bitter towards you until they have a reason to forgive you. But you would be crazy to think they should not remember you did that and not hold it against you. The other person would be crazy if they continued to stand within an arm's distance and did not hold your previous attack against you. The world is full of bitterness, and much of it is justified. So, instead of being ignorant of that reality, maybe we should teach that we should seek redemption to ameliorate the bitterness others may have towards us.

But when it comes to your spouse, you should not be bitter. Why? Because you have both taken a vow to work for the betterment of each other. In other words, your spouse vowed to build you up, not poison you. Yes, there will be times when you hurt each other, but you must take into consideration all things when dealing with determining how you should feel about someone. When it comes to your spouse, the vows they took to aim for your betterment should supersede all other concerns.

Perhaps we ought to make our vows clearer. We ought to say a vow to always pursue the other's betterment and a vow to trust that our spouse will do the same. That way, we can always forgive and trust them, and they can do the same.

MATHEMATICS OF LOVE

When you are married, you should not keep a record of wrongs; otherwise, it will lead to bitterness. You should not be pondering that they might not be good enough or have failed too many times. No, you should find serenity in the fact that they have vowed to actively try their best to love you and be a good spouse regardless of what you do. They may mess up, but they are trying, and that is what they promised when you married. So, forgive them. Immediately. Completely. Do not hold their mistakes against them because they have decided to be there for you forever. They may screw up time and time again, but as long as they are trying to follow the right path that is sufficient for forgiveness (the atonement need not be repaid either as you are both *one* now, and what is yours is theirs and what is theirs is yours).

Now, if they are cruel and unrepentant for their wrongdoings, then tell your spouse they are not acting in the way they should. If they truly meant their vows, they will do their best to work with you to pursue what is right. Sometimes, it may take a while for someone to come around, for our faults are not always obvious or easy to judge. However, as the contract of marriage has been drawn, you can assume they are deserving of mercy and forgiveness because you trust them.

With the act of marrying someone, you commit to loving your spouse and yourself to the best of your abilities. It is just like the relationship a Christian has with God.

"Now as the church submits to Christ, so also wives should submit in everything to their husbands. Husbands, love your wives, as Christ loved the church and gave himself up for her."
- Ephesians 5:24–25

I also find it quite interesting that the Bible gives husbands and wives separate responsibilities in marriage. Continuing in verse 33, it says *"let each one of you love his wife as himself, and let the wife see that she respects her husband."* Why is it that they have different roles? Why is it not that both partners should love each other as themselves and respect each other? Maybe, that is because it is getting at a common problem that persists in many marriages. Some men do not care enough for their wives as that they are not willing to put their wives before their careers and their own desires. Men are more prone to abuse their wives because they are generally larger and stronger and capable of doing so. On the other hand, some women are manipulative in marriage and try to take advantage of the situation. They show little respect for their husband and treat them as a child.

So, what are we to learn from all of this? If you are an unmarried man, find someone who is not manipulative and is trustworthy and will respect you even when she has the upper hand. You must actually believe that your spouse is trustworthy because you must always believe that she truly understood and meant what she said when she vowed that she will always aim for the betterment of the two of you.

A woman should look for a man who cares for her as he does for himself, if not more. Know that when you are married, you are to be full of forgiveness for your spouse; therefore, find someone who is not likely to take advantage of such mercy. Most importantly, do not get married unless you believe that you fit the proper role and your significant other fits their respective role.

If there was a circuit board with switches for justice and mercy it would seem that only one can be turned on at a time. Marriage requires turning off justice and turning the mercy and grace switch on, closing the control panel, locking it up and throwing away the key. Marriage is 100% mercy and grace.

Marriage (or any covenant) is the foundation for the virtue of faith.

Friendship is the foundation for the virtue of trust.

To be clear, marriage is not closing your eyes and willingly blinding yourself to your partner's shortcomings. It is taking all things into consideration, including the vows of marriage. Marriage is believing and trusting that each person sincerely recited their vows and that those vows are sufficient to supersede all things.

As I have previously stated, to give up justice is to give up the motivation people have to work hard and aim for greatness. However, in marriage, both people are vowing to aim for the betterment of each other, and therefore the marriage can survive 100% forgiveness as each person will continue to have a proper aim despite the ability for someone to take advantage of the forgiveness.

Some will see this analysis of marriage and think it is beautiful that someone would sign up for such a thing. And then we realize the responsibility we are taking upon ourselves and how terrifying it is. Marriage is no joke. It's not easy. It's hard work. And yet most walk blindly into it because they are told it is categorically good. It is good if you go about it wisely and devastating if you walk into it without an understanding of what marriage actually requires.

MODERN CHURCH

If someone attacks you, you will hold that against them and not be so close to them the next time you see them. Yet, churches still preach that we should forgive and not hold them accountable, or they say things such as *"Forgive them in your heart, but you can still hold them accountable."*

They do not differentiate between unconditionally forgiving your spouse and conditionally forgiving the rest of the world. Therefore, we treat our spouses like any other relationship where we hold them accountable for their wrongdoings. What a travesty! We hold bitterness against our spouses and fail to forgive them even though we pretend that we are forgiving them in our hearts. It means nothing to only forgive your spouse in your heart. People only care that you forgive them by treating them as if their shortcoming never happened. Until you do that, the bitterness will remain. And there should be no bitterness in marriage.

What else can you expect when you put two people in the same home for a lifetime? They will fight and surely both parties will have shortcomings. The old way of marriage, the biblical way that required unconditional forgiveness, was the only thing that kept the bitterness completely out of marriage.

But do we preach forgiveness properly? Or do we preach that we should apply forgiveness to everyone equally?

We take the one earthly relationship that supposed to be a resemblance of the divine and beautiful, and we have brought it down to the level of all other relationships. We are bitter about them and think that they might be the same for us. We have taken the one relationship that resembles a divine relationship where forgiveness is freely given and treat it as if it was any other relationship where we still hold people accountable for their actions.

We have killed marriage. We have created a new idea and stolen the glorious name of the old. Marriage is dead. We have taken the one institution on earth that has the ability to resemble something divine, and we have prostituted it. We can see the carnage. The divorces and bitterness lie all around us.

We still speak of the old marriage as if it exists, but we do not search for it. We say that we want a *match made in heaven*, yet we do not even bother to look at the one relationship we have with a Being in heaven to see how such a relationship can exist.

Was it not enough for people to just kill their God by saying that He was no longer believable? Why must we kill all that we have in His name, even that which is good?

Do you wish to kill something simply because it has an association with something you do not like? Where will that stop? Shall we kill the virtue of *love* next because God promoted that too? Shall we kill all of the virtues for they all can be improper at times? Shall we kill those who actually have a bit of the transcendence in them?

The thought that marriage is no longer viable has been played out before us. We have seen the drama of our newly invented marriage play out on stage. We have seen actors slain and lying on the stage as they slowly bleed out from the wars that took place between couples that claimed to trust each other at the altar, but did not know what they were saying. Some of the audiences have begun to let the play's story seep into their philosophy as stories of failed marriages perpetually play on every other stage. And what other conclusions should they draw when they see something so toxic in front of them?

It only makes sense for them to forgo their belief in the barbaric institution that we now call marriage.

To be an individual and to think for yourself does not mean that you must do things differently than the past or what others currently do. It means that you think about what is ideal and pursue it. Sometimes, others are properly pursuing an ideal and you should do the same, but when others pursue that which is not ideal, the greater man veers off and pursues the ideal.

The old ways, which I believe were ideal, are still played out on some stages, but the viewers no longer attend those old plays for they do not sing songs as sweet and comforting. The harsh realities of the old marriage do not have as many scripted soundbites that can be posted as advertisements for the world to see.

And if the old ways have disappeared completely from all stages, we can still open books and find the script, if we truly search hard enough.

IN LOVE

The words "*I love you*" carry a weight incomparable to most utterances that one can say. The first time it is said, the world seems to change for the person hearing it. Perhaps, the only words more important are "*I do.*"

The words "*I love you*" mean something just as the words "*I do*" mean something. Sadly, however, most men say it for the first time without understanding what they are getting themselves into.

A woman sees the words "*I love you*" as a symbol of the relationship moving forward and closer to marriage. A woman sees it as a necessary step before an engagement. A woman sees a man say "*I love you*" in a movie and they soon marry. And if the relationship were to abruptly end, the woman will feel betrayed. She will be devastated because she had thought that when he said, "*I love you,*" it meant that they had a bond stronger than one that could break so easily. Women tend to have a more consensual understanding of what it means to them than males do.

A man sees the words *"I love you"* as one of a hundred things. It could be something done out of desperation that keeps the relationship afloat. It could mean that you want to spend forever with her. It could be a way to manipulate the woman into believing that the relationship is further along than it is. It could also mean that he feels a momentary state of joy.

Perhaps, you shouldn't tell someone you are in love with them until you are at the point where the relationship can be treated as marriage with only one exception. The only exception is that you will judge if they take advantage of your mercy and grace.

When you are in love, and not yet married, it means that you are willing to no longer judge them with justice but with mercy, as long as they stay within the bounds of the assumed relationship. It is telling the woman that you are at the point where you stop keeping a record of wrongs and just work for the betterment of each other and mercy flows freely. And if they do not take advantage of that situation, then proceed to marriage where there will be no judging at all.

It is a test run for marriage where each partner can experience what the other person will do when they are married.

'*I love you*' is a statement of great meaning. The relationship is in a new place, and it has moved forward. Women tend to subconsciously know what it means, yet men can have a different understanding. It should be discussed what it means to be in love. The words mean so much, yet we never actually discuss what they mean or explain what they mean to each of us individually.

When to Marry

Leaving feelings, mercy and justice aside, practically speaking, when is the ideal time to marry?

How can you stay up late working on a new business idea when you have a family and partner waiting for you after work? It's extremely difficult to get the ball moving when your time and energy are also being taken up by your marriage and family. When you are single, you have much more time to devote to ventures that are crucial for sustenance.

Try to hold off marriage until you have some footing in the world.

First, aim to be invested in something that puts you a step ahead. Growth is often exponential, and the first step is often the largest and takes the most effort. Therefore, get the ball rolling. Once you believe you are on the path to what you want and can bear the responsibility of marriage, then look for a spouse. So, get your degree, put in long hours to get that promotion, learn a valuable skill and experiment where others do not dare. Invest in yourself now, so that you have the freedom to continue pursuing your desires while you are married.

Marriage is a grand responsibility that we should not take lightly. Some responsibilities are so great that they take up all our time and disallow us from growing in other areas of our lives that need tending to. Marriage is a grand responsibility, so make sure that when you are married, you can handle it without *completely* compromising your other responsibilities.

"The unmarried man is anxious about the things of the Lord, how to please the Lord. But the married man is anxious about worldly things, how to please his wife, and his interests are divided."
- 1 Corinthians 7:32–34
"I do not think you can name many great inventions that have been made by married men."
- Nikola Tesla[7]

I would say that we should aim to marry someone at some point in our lives. But we should only take such an aim when the time is proper. Be virtuous and do not blindly rush into something because you are told to or because you are pressured to. Let your passions motivate you but use your conscience to help you determine when and whom you should marry.

How to Love in a Marriage

How many weddings have you been to where the following beautiful verses are read?

"Love is patient and kind; love does not envy or boast; it is not arrogant or rude. It does not insist on its own way; it is not irritable or resentful; it does not rejoice at wrongdoing, but rejoices with the truth. Love bears all things, believes all things,

hopes all things, endures all things.
Love never ends."
- 1 Corinthians 13:4–8

While beautiful and uplifting, the reality is that the aforementioned verses do not apply to the way a husband should *act* towards his wife. The word for *love* used is the Greek word *agapē*, which is the desire to have a relationship with someone if they are trustworthy. People often think that these verses are ways in which the spouses will treat each other, but it actually relates to the mindset of relationships— the desire to establish and maintain proper relationships. Marriage is one that has already been permanently established and that you have vowed to forever maintain.

When the verse says that *agapē* should not insist on its own ways that does not mean that you should affectionately love someone by not insisting on your own ways. It means that you should not insist that someone change to become someone you can trust, but you should rejoice when they turn from evil and become someone you can trust. In the same way, we should not insist that our enemies change, but we should rejoice when they do change. There will be times when you should actually insist on your ways being done, but you should not insist someone changes to meet your standards. In fact, your wife should already meet your standards and you should already trust her and that part of the description of *agapē* is essentially irrelevant in application towards your spouse. I wonder how many have told their spouse, *"You must not insist on doing it your way because you love me."*

Should you always be patient with your spouse? No, sometimes you need to put your foot down and stop the chaos. But you should always be steadfast in your hope that another person (non-spouse) will change and meet your standards for friendship. The verses applies to the mindset one should have in approaching a relationship, not how you will act towards one another.

I wonder how many have told their spouse, *"You must be patient with me in my wrongdoings because you love me."* I wonder how many spouses have told their spouse, *"You must bear what I am doing because you love me."*

And yes, I know that the Bible also mentions that "*husbands should [agapē] their wives*," but we need to look at the context.

"In the same way husbands should agapē their wives as their own bodies. He who agapēs his wife loves himself. For no one ever hated his own flesh, but nourishes and cherishes it."
- Ephesians 5:28–29

The first sentence states that a husband should desire to have a proper relationship with himself and his wife. The second that the husband should treat himself and his wife equally because they are both one. It then implies in the third sentence that the two of them have met their own standards and should now treat each other as if they were someone they cared about as much as themselves. This makes sense because the husband has decided to permanently have a relationship with his wife as she has met his standards, and therefore, he should now care for her and aim for her betterment. And, as the two are one, the husband must also treat himself in such a way.

In short, desire to have a proper relationship with your wife and yourself as you should trust your wife (and, therefore, yourself as you are now one). A proper relationship consists of desiring their betterment and affectionate love for one another.

Being married is becoming one. The way you cared about yourself and planned out your life prior to being married should change to now include your spouse as if they were also you. Marriage is not about caring about another person more than yourself; it is caring about both of you equally.

It does not mean you *treat your wife* with the virtues stated in 1 Corinthians 13 but to *treat the relationship* you have with your wife in such a way. In other words, when someone meets your standards for trust (which you and your wife do), then have an affectionate love for yourself and for your wife. It means to truly desire the betterment in the other person and to be willing to suffer for them if needed for their betterment. That is how we ought to love those we choose to have a relationship with. It is treating your spouse as yourself because you two are one. And if you do not treat your spouse as someone you truly care about, then you are not caring for who you are.

But this does not mean you should be happy with who you currently are. This does not mean that you should lavish yourself in royalties because you are in love with yourself.

Affectionate love is slightly more complicated than blindly following a few prescribed virtues. We will dive into what love actually looks like in the fifth chapter. But know that the love we talk about in Chapter 5 will be only for those you believe meet your standards of trust and friendship. It is not to be given to everyone, for love is difficult. It takes hard work. It often requires the willingness of suffering for the betterment of someone, and it should not be given freely to those who will not be proper stewards of your love.

Betterment of Each Other

I have said that when we marry, we take a vow to desire the betterment of the other spouse and the relationship. But you must also realize that you and your spouse are now one.

You are vowing to work for the betterment of your spouse (and, therefore, you are included in that idea). It is implied that you are also vowing to aim for your own betterment. It is not only a vow to be a loving spouse but also a vow to say that you are on a path of aiming to be better and to continually better yourself and become the best person you can be.

Marriage is, by its very nature, anti-nihilistic. The act of marrying is a statement that says that you and I are worth loving and are valued. It is saying that we are worth living for. It is pushing away nihilistic philosophy and vowing to devote yourself to work for the betterment of your spouse and yourself.

CHAPTER 4

"Courage is resistance to fear, mastery of fear—not absence of fear. Except a creature be part coward it is not a compliment to say it is brave; it is merely a loose application of the word."
- Mark Twain[1]

On Edge

Anxiety

With all this talk about men of high character, I would like to say that I can relate to Indiana Jones…at least on one level—I am terrified of snakes. As I traveled through Central America in 2018, I found myself on the west coast of Costa Rica in the province of Guanacaste. One day, I went walking for supplies, which lead me to a narrow path through an enclosed jungle area. As I approached the jungle path, I noticed a dead snake lying near the entrance. Despite its inability to harm me, I still detoured to go around the carcass. After I passed the carcass, a thought consumed me; my eyes widened with fear as I realized that I would be walking through a jungle path, not more than three feet wide, for the next half mile. All I could think of were snakes hiding along the trail and waiting to leap up at me. I analyzed every step and scanned constantly for anything that resembled a snake. Every suspicious-looking tree branch made my adrenaline spike. I was hyper-focused, searching for any snake or predator that might bring me harm.

As the trail began to widen and the overgrowth no longer covered the ground, my anxiety reduced. It's not that snakes were any less likely to appear where I walked, but now I knew I was more capable of dealing with a snake as I had more visibility and if I were to see one, I would have more time to react. Even in the wide part of the trail, my fear of snakes still somewhat haunted me, but now I was in a situation where I could better cope with my fear. At the end of the trail, I emerged onto the pavement and took a deep breath and relaxed. I had survived and could continue towards the store for my supplies.

The journey through the jungle brought two thoughts to mind. First, fear is vital to survival and growth. Second, fear can initiate consciousness.

To address the first point, we should ask the questions, *should we have fears* and *how should we handle our fears?* We can do one of the following in the face of something that causes fear: 1) be paralyzed; 2) ignore the fear; or 3) be cognizant of the fear while attempting to carry out our goals.

As I stood at the entrance to the jungle path, I realized I had three options: 1) to avoid my fear and not enter; 2) to ignore my fears and walk through without regard for snakes; or 3) to be brave and cognizant.

The first option would lead to nowhere. The result would be to avoid the problem and sit at the edge of the jungle. I would avoid difficulties, temporarily avoid suffering and avoid all pain. Or I could look for another path, but another path would not be as efficient and may take a long time to traverse, only to end up at the same place.

The second option—to ignore my fears—was foolish. A comforting quote often stated by so-called wise men is to encourage people to have no fear or to ignore their fears because they only hold one back. But if you take their advice literally, that will result in you ignoring a normal human reaction and not concerning yourself with the existing dangers. You would foolishly walk into the forest with your head held high and not scan the ground for predators because you are not afraid of them. While this may relieve stress, it may get you bitten and killed if you step on the tail of a deadly snake.

The third option is only for those who believe that they are capable of accomplishing the task, find the task worthwhile or see no other option to go around and are required to reach the destination. This option will allow you to achieve your goal in an efficient manner and give you the best opportunity for survival. This entails scanning the ground feverishly and looking for deadly predators with every step you take. It's terrifying; I can attest to that. But you receive a rush of adrenaline as this bravery is rewarded by the body, allowing it to have the energy and focus to accomplish the task.

God willing, you safely accomplish your task and become more skilled at trekking the jungle path. You learn what to avoid and where the snakes may nest. The fear feels like it resides or fades with each accomplishment, but in reality, fear is always there. You only become braver and more capable of accomplishing your goal.

The more capable you are of accomplishing your goal, the less anxious you feel. As the odds of the danger overtaking you decrease, the properly functioning mind begins to reduce the amount of adrenaline needed to be conscious of these fears.

Fear is just one of the drivers of our attention. And our attention is given to anything that will help us better achieve our future goals. If our goal is happiness, we will focus on things that we expect to make us happy, such as a butterfly. If our goal is to win a competition, anything that can benefit us in preparation will catch our attention. If our goal is to survive, retain our job or achieve a daring task, we pay attention to our fears so that they do not prevent us from achieving our goal. Fear may only be an illusion, but it is an illusion that keeps us on the proper path; fear makes you aware of that which is not conducive to your wellbeing and continuation. It is the illusion that something bad might happen, and therefore, we are aware of the potential harm and in a state of *fight or flight*.

ANXIETY

Regarding the subject of anxiety, I mentioned that *option two* was less stressful or anxiety-provoking than option three. Anxiety tends to be categorically perceived as a negative characteristic; Søren Kierkegaard thought otherwise. In his book, *The Concept of Anxiety*, the 19th-century Danish philosopher wrote that "*Whoever has learned to be anxious in the right way has learned the ultimate."*[2] The proper amount of fear and anxiety is beneficial and not only useful but also natural. But to over-exaggerate our fears to the point that they are irrational creates superfluous anxiety in our life.

For example, I over exaggerate my fear of snakes. I think everything in the jungle that moves is a snake waiting to kill me. However, there is nothing behind most rocks, and in reality, most snakes are not harmful to humans. If I am uninformed of a snake's capabilities, and I run into a harmless snake, adrenaline and anxiety will rush to my mind when it is unnecessary. This could be reduced by learning the types of snakes and the truth of the circumstances. If I am informed and react with anxiety to a dangerous snake, this is optimal as anxiety can help us react more quickly if we learn how to manage it.

In 2006, Lynne Isbell published a paper titled "Snakes as Agents of Evolutionary Change in Primate Brains"[3] in the Journal of Human Evolution, which detailed a new concept called the Snake Detection Theory. The theory is based on the fact that primates' visual systems have developed more rapidly in areas where venomous snakes lurk. Primates that have co-inhabited areas that have venomous snakes developed a larger pulvinar region of the brain, which helps to detect visually relevant stimuli. She proposed that *"snakes were ultimately responsible for these defining primate characteristics."*

So, what are we to learn from this? To jump into snake pits so that we can better our eyesight? No. It is possible that a fear of snakes makes mammals develop better eyesight over time, or it may also be possible that everyone with bad eyesight died as they were not suitable to reproduce because the snakes killed them. Either of these plausible outcomes, whichever that may be, is valuable to learn from. For if it is the first option and we develop our skills due to our fears, then we should be encouraged to face our fears when we are capable of handling them. And as we continue to face them, they will become more easily accomplished because we are better suited. Or second, those who are blind to harmful things may be harmed or killed. Either way, it appears that being cognizant of dangerous things is beneficial.

RELIGIOUS ORIGINS

The religious scriptures seem to me to be more than just a fantastical story of historic events. Regardless of whether you believe them to be true, you can learn the philosophical ideas that they provide. As such, to understand the application of fear, we will be exploring the biblical story of the Garden of Eden and the beginning of the Buddha's life.

The first story of the Bible involving humans is that of Adam and Eve. Most of us know this story, even if we are not religious. A short summary of the story is that Adam and Eve were the first two humans on earth, living in the Garden of Eden. It was a place of pleasure, as even the name Eden means *pleasure*, and they could do whatever they pleased as long as they did not eat from the *"tree of the knowledge of good and evil"* (Genesis 2:17) or they would surely die. Eve is convinced by a snake to eat from the tree, and she shares the fruit with Adam. As soon as they ate from the fruit, *"the eyes of both were opened, and they knew that they were naked"* (Genesis 3:7).

When confronted by God, they were punished with new difficulties, such as pain in childbearing for the woman and difficult work for the man, which would cause him to sweat to earn the bread he needed to eat (Genesis 3:16–19). They were then cast out of the garden of pleasure and into the world as we know it today.

The first question anyone should ask at this point is: why would a snake convince Eve to eat the fruit? If the snake really represents Satan, as the idea has been proposed, why did Satan come down as a reptile? Furthermore, why was the tree so specifically named *the tree of knowledge of good and evil*?

I must say I am rather fond of the Bible's use of a snake, as it fits in well with my previous example. The story could have had any type of character really, but the use of a predator is so much more relatable to the reader. We often skip over the ideas presented by the story and just stick to the literal interpretation. We often don't understand that the snake gave the two humans the tool to become conscious—fear.

Our fears are often what lead to our consciousness. The story starts with the characters being completely unashamed of their nakedness and then becoming conscious and insecure after their interaction with the predator. Why? Because the very thought of predators reminds us that we are weak and fallible and need to be alert so that we can deal with our fallibility. After the interaction with the snake, Adam and Eve are cognizant of their body and cover themselves up with the leaves of a fig tree, as if like armor against their current inadequacy.

Why is it that the tree, which is forbidden by God, is called the tree of knowledge of good and evil? Because the fruit that the snake gives you is the awareness of things that are evil and may harm you. And when we know that there are evil harmful things, then we can also know that there are good things that will not harm us. Hence, the knowledge of good and evil. We need one to know of the other. For example, we know that the sun produces light because shadows disappear when it is not present. Would we even notice the sun's light if we never saw a shadow?

When Adam and Eve were in Eden, there was no need for fear. Everything was pleasant and nothing was dangerous. After eating from the tree, they unlocked the key to live in the real world, and as such, they would be placed in the real world where snakes bite, work is exhausting and people grow old and die. The tree produces the fruit that gives us knowledge of things that are good and evil. It creates consciousness so that we can properly fear the things that are harmful if we choose to live in a world where harm is present.

And it was not just a coincidence that the devil took the form of a terrifying predator to show that the things that harm us also bring us the fruit of consciousness.

The story of Buddha begins around 567 BC when Buddha was only a baby named Siddhartha Gautama. Twelve years before the birth of Buddha, a prophecy that he would either be a great sage (a Buddha) or a great ruler was given to his father, the king of the Shakya clan. In order to keep his son on the path of being a great ruler, the king kept the young prince from encountering any suffering or discomfort. The child stayed within the palace walls and lived a life of perfect comfort and luxury. The father only allowed healthy and caring people to interact with the child. As the young Siddhartha sat under a tree in meditation, the tree's shadow had remained motionless throughout the day to protect him from the sun. The young boy was shielded from all sickness, harm, old age and death. He lived a life of pure pleasure without any need for fear.

At the age of 29, despite his perfectly comfortable life, Siddhartha requested to go on a chariot ride outside the walls and through the rest of the city. The king allowed it but had all the sick and old people removed from the path of the prince. Despite the order, one old man was visible on the route, and Siddhartha noticed him. The chariot driver informed the sheltered prince of the concept of old age and that all would soon experience it. Siddhartha went on more excursions and encountered sickness and death for the first time. Intrigued by the real world, Siddhartha requested to leave, explore and search for something to make sense of the human suffering he had recently discovered so that he could remove all that suffering. Siddhartha went into the real world and on towards his path to becoming the enlightened Buddha.

The origin of Buddha seems to resemble much of the biblical story of the Garden of Eden. The young prince was provided a place of comfort that was void of suffering. He had one patriarchal guide who arranged the environment and kept anything that could harm him at bay. Yet, despite the perfection he inhabited, he encountered something harmful and painful and chose to not be unconscious to the dangers and realities of the world. To learn more about the reality of the good and evil in the world, he left the protected kingdom his father had prepared.

Both religious stories are tied together by the idea that humans were once in a place of perfection but have chosen to leave and explore the real world where life is not perfect and have become aware of what is good and evil. Despite the utopia in which they lived, the characters still left for a world where they could contend with the good and the evil. There is now suffering in the world, and therefore, the characters would have to find the best way to deal with it. The two religious beliefs may have different methods of going about suffering, but both give the idea that the introduction of something terrible can lead to the knowledge of good and evil. This is truly a profound idea that is found in Christianity, Islam and Buddhism.

THE SHADOW

The religious tend to look at Sigmund Freud with disapproval. And I will not debate the fact that he was wrong in certain aspects, but he did pioneer a path in psychology that led to many breakthroughs. He explored the idea of a dark side, a shadow-side that is primitive and innate within us. Carl Jung furthered the idea of the *shadow*, which can be described as the dark side or the untapped potential of our personality. For example, we see the shadow when a celebrity does something terrible and says in pity, "*It was not like me to do that stupid thing*," because they do not usually partake in those dark things or ever imagined they were even capable of doing something horrendous. Honestly, to say "*that was not like me*" only shows that they still won't face the reality of who they truly are and are unwilling to actually grow from that situation. What they ought to say is, "*I did not realize that I was capable of such a horrendous act. I now know that I am capable of such a dark thing, and I will try to understand why I did it and how I got to that place, so I never do such a terrible thing again.*"

Most people tend to accept the idea that there is good and evil within everyone. Yet, many do not believe that they themselves are capable of evil or that they could ever do something so terrible. The idea of the shadow is not for when things are going well but to prevent evil from occurring when things are not.

It sounds strange to contemplate the evil within you so that you can learn how to handle it. We are told that they are things to stay away from, to not let them come across your path if you want happiness; however, the truth is that we must embrace these dark and gloomy ideas and understand how to handle them if we want to best manifest ourselves in the future we hope to obtain. For it is better to plan for our future and prepare for a disaster than to hope it all works out and blindly steer our lives.

It is vital to examine the worst parts of our lives. You don't have to share it with everyone but do understand what brings you to that point. Understand what enticed you to partake in something you are not proud of. Understand it so you can be cognizant of the warning signs when they encroach on your life again so you can prepare yourself in advance on how you want to handle the situation and do not fall into the same trap again.

There is always the potential for evil. We must try desperately to understand what might allow that evil to succeed in ruling so that we do not have to encounter it again. That is virtuous. That is good.

That's why we examine the potential darkness within us. We ought not to say we are incapable of evil—because we are. We are seriously capable of terrible evils. So, learn what evils are within you and determine how you can prevent them from occurring.

It's similar to the idea of learning history so that you do not have to repeat it. It's always easier to look at something else and critique it rather than looking within yourself. It means searching within your mind to see what thoughts come up which may be leading you down a bad road. Most would rather have ignorant bliss than to consider that they might be making the same mistake that so many others have made. Half of the reason we are taught to understand history is to learn about the terrible atrocities that have occurred in the past so we can look for signs of leading towards that in the present and prevent evil. But rarely are we taught to look within ourselves to prevent us from doing terrible things.

Obviously, it's more difficult to look within yourself. Millions have examined wars and can confirm the events and agree with others; within you, it is more ambiguous. But that does not mean that you should not try.

IGNORING FEAR

As stated above, one of the three reactions to fear is pretending that fear does not exist. You can say that fear is only an illusion and should be ignored. To pursue a noble goal without any regard for fears can be found in many popular quotes that are being repeated time and again as though they are golden ideas to follow. Below, I have listed a few that I found compelling but lacking in substance.

"America was not built on fear. America was built on courage,
on imagination and an unbeatable determination to do the job
at hand."

- President Harry S. Truman[4]

But fear sure became a handy excuse when Truman dropped atomic bombs that killed tens of thousands of civilians. I am not saying what he did was wrong. In Truman's public remarks after the first bomb dropped on Japan, he stated, *"Let there be no mistake, we shall completely destroy Japan's power to make war."*[4] So then, the only reasonable question is: Why? What was the purpose of destroying *"every productive enterprise the Japanese have"*?[5] Answer: Truman and his military advisers feared that an invasion from Japan would result in many US men dying. Regardless of whether it was right or wrong, I think Truman would agree that we survived on fear. I agree that America was built on courage, imagination and persistence, but I also believe that fear was an essential factor mixed into the foundation of the country.

"The only thing we have to fear is fear itself..."

- President Franklin D. Roosevelt[6]

The president preceding Truman has often been ascribed with this witty and simple quote. The quote addresses the negative aspects of fear (fear causes anxiety that petrifies), but the quote fails to see the positive aspects and the necessary reasons for fear. But, maybe, we ought to look at the whole quote from his first inaugural address to give context to the type of fear he is referring to: *"So, first of all, let me assert my firm belief that the only thing we have to fear is fear itself—nameless, unreasoning, unjustified terror which paralyzes needed efforts to convert retreat into advance."* It turns out that Roosevelt was referring to only the irrational fears that are unreasonable and unjustified, which stop us from doing the things we should do. The quote does not say you should not have fears, but only that we should not have fears of irrational things. It is a shame we use only a portion of his quote and often in the incorrect context as so many apply it to all fears. Roosevelt was right, but those who use it out of context are wrong.

Ignoring your fears is only an ideal stance to take when your fears are irrational. I would always be cautious in telling people to avoid an emotion that we have either been given by God or that has been used by humans for millions of years and has persisted in the evolutionary pool, whichever you may believe to be the case. We ought to have a fear of things that are not conducive to our wellbeing and continuation. Therefore, know which fears are truly dangerous, and if they are, then pay close attention to them.

Our bodies were designed to help us best manifest ourselves in this world. We feel fear to be alert of potential dangers. We feel pain when we are under attack. Sometimes, we should push through the pain and continue in our endeavor, while other times we should relent and yield in order to keep our body from unnecessary pain. No one should endorse ignoring all pains, for pains are an indicator of the events surrounding us so that we may then decide how to best react. No one should advocate ignoring all fears, for fears are an indicator of the dangers surrounding us, helping us decide how to best react.

Some may even use Bible verses to argue that we ought not to fear.

"Have I not commanded you? Be strong and courageous. Do not be frightened, and do not be dismayed, for the LORD *your God is with you wherever you go."*
- Joshua 1:9

We must understand the context. When do we not need to fear? When we are safe and in the presence of something that will not harm us, such as angels, under the direct protection of God (but only when God gives it to you). According to the Bible, another thing you have no need to fear, if you are a believer, is hell because salvation has already been assured. But to use this quote, which refers to a group being directed by God to go to war, out of context, may cause some to struggle with whether we ought to have fear in everyday tasks without God's appointed protection.

The greater man is fearful of that which may have a significant effect on him. He does not treat such things as if they are harmless and meaningless, but with seriousness. In the face of something powerful, he changes. It is a man of high character who comprehends the urgency and seriousness of paying attention or acting rightly, thereby being optimally prepared.

Do not be afraid of things that are not significant and hold no possibility of significantly affecting you. Have no fear that another can take away your salvation but do fear for your own life in times of peril. Fear God for He provides the air for each breath and can take it away.

FEAR GOD

> *"There is no fear in agapē, but perfect agapē casts out fear. For fear has to do with punishment, and whoever fears has not been perfected in agapē."*
>
> - 1 John 4:18

There is no fear in *agapē*, but there is fear in affectionate love. How do we reconcile the idea that "There is no fear in *agapē*, but perfect *agapē* casts out fear" (1 John 4:18) with the idea that we are to have *agapē* for God (Matthew 22:37) and also fear God (Psalm 34:9, Acts 10:35, Luke 1:50)? By starting with the proper definition of *agapē*— the desire to have a relationship with someone and doing so only if you trust them.

Our desire to have a proper friendship should not be affected by fears. No matter the strength or power or capabilities of another person that we may see as terrifying and greater than our own, we should not allow that fear to hold us back from desiring a relationship if we trust them.

For example, if we were to have an *agapē* for a pet we should still fear it if it is capable of serious harm. To look at the first point, having an *agapē* for a dog means that we should pursue a proper relationship with the dog if we trust it. Perhaps you will hear that this breed is often evil or too aggressive or untrustworthy, but you know that the dog is trustworthy and acts rightly as a pet should. Then, do not allow these fears to affect your *agapē* because your *agapē* is based on trust and not predetermined assumptions.

At the same time, the dog may be powerful and capable of ferocity, and should be feared if you abuse the dog or attack someone that the dog affectionately loves like a family member.

Therefore, do not let fear affect your desire for a proper relationship (*agapē*), but have fear of those who may significantly impact you. This is how we can have a mindset of *agapē* without fear and have the feeling of fear and love for God. Again, we must realize that *agapē* is not an action, but a mindset. Fear is an action.

Without this understanding of *agapē*, we miss the main idea—the more perfect your *agapē*, the less it is based on presupposed assumptions and more on the individual's actual character.

Have No Fear

We say "*judge not*" as if it is an absolute virtue to not have an ideal and compare other things to it. We say "*have no fear*" too, but what is the point in saying such a thing? Is it because you fear my belief is detrimental and not ideal for me? Is it not hypocritical to say "*fear not*"? For, in doing so, the person saying such a thing is fearful that if I continue to have fears then I will be stalled or completely overcome by fear. If you truly had no fear that I might be making an error or an unideal choice, you would not need to say "*fear not.*" You would not care if I had any fear for it would make no difference. But we all know that our own fears can be useful, and so we express our fears that the other person should have no fears.

To write a book that tells people not to fear, as otherwise bad things will happen, is pure hypocrisy. The only reason you would write such a book is that you fear that people who do fear are not living optimally, and they need to change to avoid fear. But by writing such a book, you are fearful of the negative consequences of fear and are warning people about it. You would be a fear-monger on the subject of being anti-fear.

To those who tell me that I should have no fears, I will tell them that they should not fear my fear.

We also judge others for judging. *The hypocrisy in telling another person that the ideal human should not have an ideal, and that we should aim to be the ideal human is laughable.* And yet, sadly, so many actually say and believe that we should not judge as if that was an absolute virtue.

We tell others to aim for our ideals but that they should not have their own ideals. To tell someone to never fear or to never judge is to take away their individuality. It is telling them to do what you think is best and to make them feel guilty for thinking for themselves.

And to those who tell me not to judge, I will ask them how they came to the conclusion that it is ideal to not judge. Surely, they must have considered the options of *judging* vs. *never judging* and, as the judge, decided to take the stance that one should never judge.

When I say 'judge', I mean that we ought to aim to discover the ideal. That does not include the power and authority to control another person or harm them if they do not meet your standards. It is merely observing the case put before you and obtaining a conclusion based on the facts that have been presented. We should judge those that we think will harm us and choose to stay away from them. We should judge those who are virtuous and choose to engage with them.

The religious man might say, "*God is the ultimate judge, and he has told me not to judge.*" The latter is not true. He has only told you to judge and expect judgment in a consistent matter and to not be hypocritical. But if you truly wish to not be a judge and refrain from thinking, then go ahead. Do not vote in an election. Do not judge when someone else is a murderer, and you are on the jury. Do not hold your children responsible when they are disobedient. Do not judge the potential spouses available and just blindly pick one. Do not judge the religions available and just follow the one you were born into. And do not ask others to judge your religion as ideal, for that would be a sin according to you.

There is a time to judge and there is a time to abstain from judging. There is a time to fear and a time to be fearless.

Courage Overshadows Fear

When it comes to fears, an important idea to remember is that our fears do not disappear over time; only our anxiety is reduced as we become more capable of accomplishing a task. We will always be afraid of certain things that ought to scare us. Holding a dangerous snake will always scare even the most trained snake handler. They may learn that they do not need to fear certain snakes, but the dangerous ones will always be feared. A snake handler will not run away in fear but brave the fear and use extreme caution, proper timing and extreme focus when handling a dangerous snake. They bring tools, such as sticks or poles, to help them in their tasks. They learn the proper techniques to keep themselves safe. They may even build up a tolerance toward venom in extreme cases. But if something can hurt you, you should always fear it. Moreover, you will develop habits that help you better prepare for danger, which will also reduce your stress and anxiety.

There is only one way to eliminate fear—by convincing yourself that the thing you fear is not capable of harm. This can be good if the fear was irrational and not needed but is a mistake if the fear is potentially dangerous. You should be afraid of potentially harmful entities and therefore aware and conscious and focused on the object that is dangerous. You can also, at the same time, be brave and carry forward with the task despite fear.

I am not saying that you should always be brave and attempt every task. Some challenges may be deadly or permanently damaging if you face them unprepared. Sometimes, being petrified and not facing the challenge is the optimal action. Many animals have been known to engage in *thanatosis*, which is the act of playing dead, in order to avoid prey. The most common example is the possum, which uses the effect to deter predators who prefer to catch live prey. The hog-nosed snake not only plays dead but also releases a deathly smelling fluid to make cats think that the snake is rotting. Even humans are advised to play dead when encountering a brown bear or grizzly bear because those bears usually attack humans only if they perceive them as a threat. If someone tells you to always be brave, then be skeptical, as they may be leading you down a path of destruction.

While stories of heroism are not made of characters who shriek and cower at difficult tasks, we must not forget that these heroes train themselves to prepare for such a task. So, we should aim to build ourselves up to face such adversities. This way, we have proper opportunities to be brave and capable to face the problems of this world, despite the fear they may instill.

What happens when we avoid the fears that we ought to face? The Bible provides a story about what happens when we avoid our fears that ought to be fought in the book of Numbers. When Moses sent 12 spies into the Land of Canaan (the land promised to the Israelites by God), 10 of the 12 came back in paralyzed fear and voted against going to the land, despite the promise of obtaining the land from God. God had just opened the seas for them to walk through and promised them this land, but now they were afraid to face an army of larger men. They were in a state of irrational fear, for they were guaranteed victory as they had the power of God with them. And what was the result of this? They were forced to walk in the desert for 40 years. Wasting time, getting nowhere, only to wander in the desert and to return to the same place 40 years later for a new generation to bear the burden and fight. That is a lesson we should learn regardless of our religious beliefs.

FEAR AND RESPECT

In my travels to Panama, I was lucky enough to tour the Zapatillas Island, a picturesque national park, and had some time to explore the island. I was feeling good, so I decided to swim out to three little islands about 75–100 meters from the shore of the main island. I knew there was a small current, but I figured it would not be a big issue for me as I have previously swum much farther distances. So, I swam towards the islands. After crossing 20 meters, I began to see coral underneath me. Then fish, some a whole foot long, began to appear. It was beautiful and made me happy as I continued on my journey. As I approached the islands, a little tired from fighting the current, I realized that shallow coral surrounded the island, making it unwise to attempt to get on top of the islands. So, I immediately began my swim back.

I noticed that with every stroke forward, I would be moved further to the left than I did forward. The current was pulling me, and I began to tire from fighting it. I felt like giving up as I became exhausted. I could not rest as the current would pull me further away. So, I swam on. My shoulders began to ache as it seemed like each stroke made no difference in getting me closer to the shore.

After what seemed like an eternity, I passed over the coral and the sand became visible again. I finally had a place to put my feet down and relax. I walked up to the palm trees and then laid down, completely exhausted. I contemplated what I had done. I had newfound respect for the ocean and the currents. In fact, I had no desire to go swimming for the next week. When I did enter the ocean next, I was more cognizant of the current and would consider the speed before jumping into a similar situation in the future. I had developed a proper fear of the ocean, and I respected it because I knew it was capable of harming me.

The Bible contains more than 30 verses that make a reference to fearing God. Fearing God seemed to contradict the mainstream teaching that the world now teaches—*fear is bad*. For if this perfect deity was only good, what is there to fear in Him? Why is it that the fear of God is the beginning of wisdom? If we are on God's side, why must we fear Him? Shouldn't He be the loving father that provides for us?

First, the idea that God is on our side is not biblical. In the Old Testament, a book called Joshua contains the story of Joshua leading the Israeli army to the walled city of Jericho, where God commanded them to overtake the city. As the army rested near the town of Jericho, preparing for an upcoming battle, Joshua had the following encounter with God:

> *"Now when Joshua was near Jericho, he looked up and saw a man standing in front of him with a drawn sword in his hand. Joshua went up to him and asked, 'Are you for us or for our enemies?'*
>
> *'Neither,' he replied, 'but as commander of the army of the Lord I have now come.' Then Joshua fell facedown to the ground in reverence, and asked him, 'What message does my Lord have for his servant?'"*
>
> - Joshua 5:13–14

The first word at the beginning of the second paragraph says it all. Some biblical translations use the words *no, nay* or *neither*, but it is clear by any of the words that God was not fond of siding with an army, even when He was directing that army in their path. A wise choice of wording by God, as we humans often mistakenly believe we are on God's side or the side of goodness. The reality is that God is not backing us up regardless of what we do.

I think the lesson here is that we should not claim that God is on our side, and therefore, we are righteous. Instead, we ought to pursue what is righteous and true, or as religious people would say *"the side that God is on."* Churches and religious people will too often say that God is on their side and will get them through tough times. It seems to me to be a rather bold statement to claim to know what God will do or what He wishes would succeed, for even God allowed the life of the Old Testament character Job to fall apart.

We often change our views or realize that we did not know the full context until years later, and only then do we begin to understand that we may not have been on God's side. We expect God to follow us around simply because we said a prayer to Him. The truth is an unmovable rock that you should run towards; grapple with the steep cliffs and scrape your insufficient theories on the edges until you summit as a stronger and more capable man.

So, we may not be on God's side, but why should we fear a God or entity that is good? Because we should fear all that is greater than us and can have a significant impact on our lives. Therefore, fear God, act as you should and take his capabilities seriously.

Should You Live in Fear?

It is ideal to live in a state that allows us to best reach our desires and goals. Therefore, we may be in states of fear at times of danger and pay attention to the things that help us attain our desires. These are things that capture our attention and keep us engaged in life.

I wish I could tell you to live without fear, but the world is full of terrible and dark things, and therefore, you should be cognizant, aware and awake. Being in fear is taxing. It takes a toll on the body. Therefore, after battling out your day and facing your fears, take time off to rest and recover in a place with little anxiety. Do not live in anxiety through every moment of the day, but do not go out of your way to avoid all the fears in your life.

We need fear to stay awake and complete difficult tasks. It's the very reason so many drink coffee or tea in the morning. Caffeine sends signals along the same neural pathways that our body uses during the *fight or flight* response. We drink caffeine so that we feel fear. Society preaches that fear is bad, but we ritually use fear to wake ourselves up so we can focus on the mundane tasks the day brings. Fear, when managed properly, makes us alert and ready to face whatever challenges come our way.

You should aim to live in a manageable amount of fear. You want to have one foot in the realm of chaos, a proper amount you can handle, so that you are expanding, growing, learning and aiming at the noble and admirable. And you should keep your other foot in order, the structure that you know is safe and well-designed that keeps you from being paralyzed with fear. Once the new chaos you are encountering becomes sorted out and becomes a useful structure, then you have both feet in order. At that point, take half a step into more chaos, and then repeat. It's what keeps you awake and alert and conscious. Being in fear means you are facing the unknown and that can be the ideal when you are capable of bearing such a burden.

Fear is one thing that allows you to be alert and conscious of what the future may hold. To live in fear is to live consciously. So, aim to move forward, taking one step further into chaos, and embrace the change that is meaningful and that you are capable of handling.

Fear is the proper state you should be in when entering a chaotic or unknown situation. When there is no structure already established, there is potential for great or terrible things to occur. You do not know if you will be harmed, but there is a possibility of harm. There is a possibility for good or evil, and you need to be alert and aware to decipher if you should be in a fight or flight mode or if you can stay and gain something valuable.

Once you make the unknown situation familiar or once you structure the chaos and make order out of it and realize it is safe, then you can reduce your anxieties. You can rationally say that nothing in this room is a giant monster that may kill you, so you rationally remove certain fears.

The place may be nice to relax, rest, recover and enjoy for a short period of time, but will become a bore as we long for some new chaos in our life. We want to be surprised, to feel our heart rate increase, to truly live and grow. Not only will we long for chaos then, but the old structures may also fall apart. Material objects, knowledge and friendships will all deteriorate and diminish unless watered with the chaos of life, so we must continue building and growing so that we not only keep up with the deterioration but exceed it.

Things do fall apart, and therefore, you need to get good at making the unknown known. Heaven is the only place where things won't fall apart. But here on earth, things will fall apart, so prepare yourself to be capable of handling the chaos. Don't just wait for them to fall apart and then cry because everything is ruined. Build up what is useful. This would include not only money but also knowledge, relationships, wealth and trust. To grow these things, you must take on the responsibility of bearing a manageable amount of chaos, which will be best handled if you have a manageable amount of fear.

Fear is the byproduct of confronting chaos.

Chaos can provide the potential for growth and fear enables us to handle the chaos optimally. Fear of failure makes some people work with urgency and efficiency. For others, the stress of failure causes a mental breakdown. Often, hardship at one point in your life may serve as the fruit of good and evil that equips you with the knowledge of what may come and make you motivated to strive to never have to encounter that hardship again.

If there is nothing to fear, then there can be no growth. So, if you want to grow, then learn how to handle your fears properly instead of ignoring them.

You should not aim to live in the same anxiety you live in currently. You should aim to become more capable of taking on your current fears so that your stress is decreased to the point that you do not have stress and anxiety due to fear.

You should aim to ameliorate the current stress due to fears you have and then take on new meaningful responsibilities that will bring new fears and new stress, but then soon afterward, you will want to reduce the anxiety of those fears too.

You do not want to remove all things that cause fear and anxiety unless those things are meaningless. The fears that relate to meaningful pursuits ought to be wrestled with and subdued.

FEAR & LOVE

To have no anxiety at all means that you have subdued all your worries. But that also means that you are lacking a current challenge and a drive to obtain something or someone that you desire. If life is too easy for too long, then we become complacent and bored. A break from stress is good, but we must also remember to reinvest ourselves in the fight of pursuing something meaningful.

Fear is as essential and helpful in pursuing a goal as courage is. Fear helps us best love. Fear is not hating; it is the awareness of potential harms that may detract us from our goal. If we love something, then we fear anything that may detract us from our love.

To avoid rational fears is to avoid love. Why must we hold the stigma that fear is for those who hate? It is for those who love.

When we are aware of our problems, we can face them. But it must start with fear to make us conscious. We must stop this nonsense that fear and love cannot co-exist. Fear, when rational, is valuable, if not essential, in the process of love. So, do not dismiss the idea of fear, but instead, learn how to properly handle your fears so that you can love in the best manner possible.

NOVELTY

Our attention is given to anything that will help us better manifest our future goals. We not only pay attention to the things that better us but also the things that may detract us from our goal. Things that are novel and unique also grab our attention because we have not incorporated these unknown experiences into our framework. They might be able to fit into our framework and help us grow, they might harm us, or they might be of no value. However, as they have the potential to help, we focus our attention on that which is novel.

To directly address fear is the best way to reduce the anxiety associated with fear. We have the fear regardless, and looking directly at the fear actually allows us to reduce anxiety because then you can determine how to handle that fear. That's why scary movies are terrifying. The worst part is before the monster is visible, before you see the true embodiment of the fear. That's why horror movies are often dark—you can't see the thing you fear, and you imagine the worst possible evil lurking. When it finally becomes fully visible, it tends to disappoint, as it is not the worst possible fear we imagined. The novel things that we are yet to explore are the places that may hold the tools we need to achieve our goals, but they may also contain potential horrors that we have not yet quantified.

Often, new things are feared. Novel ideas may help us grow, but they can also be scary and dangerous. They are the unknown territory we are yet to explore and understand. We do not need to push away all novelty, but we should determine if the novelty is worthwhile before embracing it.

What we fear is chaos. But that does not mean we should always avoid chaos. It simply means we should be alert in the time of chaos and dare to encounter it if we deem it to be worthwhile.

"To venture causes anxiety, but not to venture is to lose one's self...And to venture in the highest is precisely to be conscious of one's self."
- Søren Kierkegaard[7]

FEAR TO CONSCIOUSNESS

When we become afraid, our body reacts. Our heart rate increases, adrenaline spikes, eyes widen and pupils dilate, the passageway for air into our lungs increases and our breathing accelerates. Our bodies do this naturally, particularly the amygdala of the brain, which releases stress hormones, so that we may be in the prime position to handle our fears if we choose to bravely face them. We have the extra boost of energy to scan the ground quickly and process more information in a shorter amount of time. We are able to escape more efficiently or fight with more ferocity. In short, fear allows us to better attempt to handle things that may harm us if we choose to face the fear.

We are not only afraid of things that are predatory but also of anything that may cause us distress or harm. It can be the fear of a predator attacking, having a significant other leave, failing a test, falling off the edge of a cliff or another driver crashing into you at an intersection. There could also be a fear of harm occurring to something that we love or anything that further distances us from our goals.

Therefore, we pay attention to things that may harm us. If we are driving and reaching for something in the back seat and realize we haven't looked at the road for too long a period, our body becomes fearful of what the results may be. We snap back up quickly with a greater focus than when we normally drive. Then, when we gain an understanding of the new situation, given that it is safe and nothing bad looks like it will happen, we release the anxiety as that is the rational thing to do.

The prefrontal cortex and hippocampus aid the brain in analyzing potential threats by determining if a threat is rational (truly potentially dangerous). If these two areas deem no real threat, they affect the inhibitory pathways to reduce the effects of stress hormones. In other words, the stress hormones are always reacting to anything that is dangerous, but when you consciously understand that you do not need to be anxious, the body reduces the effects of the hormone.

Therefore, open your eyes so that the hippocampus can do its job and verify the reality of the situation. Otherwise, you will assume the worst and will always be anxious even when it is not needed. This is why our fears never disappear; only our hippocampus becomes better at calming them when they are not a likely threat.

FEAR-MONGERING

We need to stop thinking that having anxiety is inherently bad.

I often hear people shut down others' comments by saying that they are fear-based or are fear-mongering. It is a term used to make someone look immature for being fearful. But that is not always right. Sometimes, our concerns should be fear-based. Sometimes, we should react out of fear.

Instead of debating whether the person who is fearful is rational, they are merely called something derogatory and ignored. They assign them a term that ends with "*phobia*" and do not consider if the fear is truly rational or not. To have a phobia is to have an irrational fear, but those who do not want to debate if it is rational or not seem to enjoy applying the term *phobia* to anything they defend. It is not wrong to fear a movement if the movement is truly dangerous.

What if someone told you that you had a *Naziphobia*? Does it make you question your dislike of Nazis? Does it make you think that you should not fear an entire group of people who believe something evil because you should not have a phobia? The truth is, it is not a phobia. It is rational to be afraid of the Nazis. Yet, people will apply *phobia* to the end of any group to make you feel guilty for being afraid of them. When someone says that you have a phobia, then respond rationally and explain your fear. If you cannot explain the fear, then perhaps it is a phobia. If you actually have no fear, but just think it is not the ideal, this is neither a phobia nor a fear. Just a judgement.

Anxiety is a virtue. Learn to use the anxiety for good as great athletes use the *fight or flight* state to excel. Anxiety can be terrible and paralyze you when you ought to move. Learn to become capable of utilizing it properly and optimally.

Some say that humans are driven and guided by fear. Most are, but not all. The greater man is driven and guided by fear as well as imagination. The weaker man only bases his life on *fear*. The weaker man waits till death and destruction are looming and then he finally gets up and tries to run away from it. The greater man does the same when fear looms, but he also opens his eyes during times of contentment, imagines a greater world and chases it.

Another type of weaker man will say that he never fears and only uses his imagination to move him. This man is crazy. He is the one who stands in the face of his death and does not react to fear. While this sounds noble, it is a childish dream, for we may be harmed if we do not react to fears.

A man of high character responds to potentially harmful fears, but is also moved by his imagination of a greater future when times are calm.

"The Wise do at once what the Fool does at last."
- Baltasar Gracian[8]

CHAPTER 5

"To say 'I love you' one must first know how to say the 'I.'"
- Ayn Rand[1]

Clinging to Conduciveness

Affectionate Love and Hate

In this chapter, we will address affectionate love. *Philia* (brotherly love), *storge* (love for a parent or a child) and *érōs* (romantic love) hold a special place in everyone's heart. This is the kind of *love* we mean when we tell our friend we love them, when we say that we love our favorite sports team or when we say that we romantically love someone.

When we say we love someone, we are saying we value them, care for their wellbeing and want the best for them. When we say we love someone, we are saying that our goal is to see the thing we love to grow and improve. In short, we love someone by helping them pursue their instincts.

It's like when you are a baby; you know you are loved because others care for you and help you when you are helpless. Even when you cannot feed, clean and shelter yourself, people love you and care for you. They want you to grow up to be a strong adult. So, they suffer sleepless nights. They feed, clean and shelter you. They are helping you grow and survive. You are their goal. You have experienced love.

Today, so many of us say we want to love or that we do love someone or something but often do not truly mean what we say.

Maybe, it's because we don't understand what love means. Love (the feeling) is the natural reaction to cling to that which contributes to our advancement, enhancement, growth and survival. Love (the action) is the willingness to sacrifice for someone so that they grow.

Love is not only the hope that good things will happen but the willingness to put forth an effort so that growth can occur. The action of love requires the willingness to sacrifice so that the thing you love can grow. Sometimes love requires sacrifice and sometimes it requires nothing.

We often portray love as easy, euphoric, comfortable and natural. Sometimes it is, but sometimes it requires sacrifice. Sacrifice can be difficult, brutal and uncomfortable.

Those who dare to love greatly do not always have easy, comfortable lives. Men of high character love so deeply that they are willing to die for those they love.

Love is not suffering for whatever someone else wants. It's willing to suffer for what is *truly best for them.*

POWER OF LOVE

Love is an addiction. It's a passion that mutes some of the sufferings in the body. Love is what makes the suffering we endure worthwhile. Without a purpose, desire, love and want for betterment, the suffering of life is bittering and meaningless.

Love is willing to bear the pain that desire requires so we can obtain our goal. This can often be detrimental when a person's passions are hard drugs or alcohol, and we ignore the slow decay of the body. An addiction can be useful when it is aimed at something good that creates growth like bearing a heavy burden in order to achieve a meaningful and noble goal. Some of the greatest inventors and artists would often find themselves mesmerized and only focus on the thing that they loved. They would forget to eat, take care of themselves or notice the outside world because they were devoted and committed to the thing they loved. They put the thing they loved as the most meaningful thing in their lives. But we must remember to rationally decide what is most meaningful and make sure that whatever is most meaningful in our life has top priority.

Have you ever heard someone comment that a vain person is *in love* with himself? That phrase seems to capture the idea of what it means to be *in love*. We know that the person who is *in love* with himself puts his own needs before anything or anyone else. And while it is good to love yourself (in the sense of being willing to suffer for the betterment of yourself), it is also noble and admirable to suffer for others. Not all the time, however, for there is a time to love others and a time to hate others.

You should suffer first for yourself. Build up your qualities, your skills and your character. Then, when you are able to fully support yourself, go out into the world and be willing to love others if they are willing to love you.

SELFISHNESS

Ayn Rand was undoubtedly a controversial author and philosopher. One of her books was *The Virtue of Selfishness*. Rand was a proponent of people who did what was best for themselves. She found it immoral to say that we should help others but not ourselves.

She presented some legitimate ideas. If we help others, shouldn't we also be allowed to help ourselves? Why is it that we should put the community and others before ourselves? Should we truly value ourselves less than others and build up others because they are more worthy? Is that not the root of communism and socialism? It is.

Rand was right that selfishness is a virtue. But she is wrong in saying that selfishness is always ideal. There are times when it is proper to be selfish. And there are times when it is proper to be loving to others and make sacrifices for them. Neither should be forced upon a person. But it should be up to a person to decide which is ideal for them in each circumstance.

When a person has their own life and their family's business in order, then sacrificing for others may be what a man of high character does. Should a billionaire always continue working and earning more money for himself if he finds it more meaningful to try to solve a humanitarian problem? I think a man of high character could choose either, depending on the details of each option he has available.

Rand thought that Jesus was a bad example of an ideal man

because he was extremely unselfish.[2] He died and was tortured so that others would be better off. Rand thought he was a fool because he was not selfish—but I disagree. I believe a man of high character knows when to be selfish and work for himself and when to take on suffering for the betterment of those he cares for. To say that we ought to only pursue one is an incomplete view of what it means to be virtuous.

Here is what I believe about selfishness: if you desire to live a selfish life where you accept no one into your world and only work for the betterment of yourself, then you have a faulty aim. We should have *agapē*, and therefore, choose to love others who we trust. Their growth is also your gain—for they are for you. Love all who are deserving of it, including yourself, your spouse, and your close friends. Do not shut out the world and be completely selfish at all times. But do aim to better yourself and those who you love.

Love and Desire

We use our imagination to visualize what the future can be for we do not desire what we already have. We ought to desire something that is greater, more beautiful, more vibrant, more long lasting, more skilled and more righteous.

A desire is created when we imagine a greater future and aim for it. Loving is the action taken to transform the present into the desired future.

We want others to love us by giving us loving actions. Yet, when we love others, we think an emotional experience ought to suffice.

Therefore, be willing to suffer for the betterment of those you love. Act in a way that shows you love them.

Love Yourself

I once met someone who was born Catholic and has since become Buddhist. He told me, "I am not a fan of Christianity because it does not tell you to love yourself. Christianity is all about helping others and repenting and focusing on changing yourself, not loving who you currently are. Buddhism makes sure that you can love yourself first so that you can love others."

But the truth is that *to love yourself* means to want yourself to be in a better place, to be willing to sacrifice for yourself so that you can grow. It doesn't mean to be content with yourself. It means to change yourself into a better person. It means to aim to be a man of high character.

When you look at it that way, Christianity does teach you to love yourself.

You can only truly feel love when you believe you are moving in the right direction. The feeling of love is the natural reaction we have to cling to that which is beneficial to our instincts. When you better yourself and grow, then you feel love for yourself.

HOW TO LOVE

How do you love a thing? How can you suffer for a song, a book or a country? Let's start with a book. You can be willing to suffer for it by paying for it. Currency is given to us in exchange for our suffering when we work. Suffering is equal to currency, and we give our currency in exchange for the book, song or whatever we find most meaningful. You may be willing to share the book with others and the ideas it contains. There are countless ways you can suffer for someone or something, and not all are equal.

When we love a flower and it grows, we are pleased. We want to see it flourish. We want to protect it and give it the right amount of light and water. Too much water can soften its roots and make it deteriorate. Too little water, and it withers away. It needs the right amount of good soil and fresh water to thrive. Too little or too much of either will kill it. To see it trampled or destroyed would sadden us.

With a person, we want to see them thrive, to shine and become not only a functional adult but one who achieves greatness and experiences great joy. A good guideline I have often heard for relationships is that if you do leave them, leave them in a better place than they began. In other words, love them.

In my travels through Panama, I briefly became friends with a lovely, free-spirited girl. She was traveling because she wanted to learn to love herself. She had some body issues in the past, so she talked about how she just wanted to love herself on this trip. We talked about what love truly was at length and came to agree on what love actually meant.

One day, we were sitting on nearby hammocks, reading books, and my friend's traveling companion came over to ask for a cigarette. My friend said she didn't have any left from the two packs they had the day before. Apparently, this was a rarity. Normally, my new friend would only smoke one or two cigarettes in a day, but now she had smoked two whole packs in a single day.

My friend volunteered to get more from the local store, but her companion was perplexed. Her companion, who was also willing to quit smoking, said, "Maybe we should not buy any more." At this point, I thought it was appropriate to chime in, as only the previous day, we had talked about the idea of love and we found that we had very similar definitions of the word love.

I asked my friend to remind me why she was traveling. She said, "To love myself, and I want to do that by enjoying myself and smoking today."

Then I asked, "How did we define love yesterday?"

"By being willing to suffer for someone so that they can be better off."

"Well then, what does it mean to love yourself?"

After pondering for a few seconds, she replied, "To be willing to suffer to better myself."

It finally dawned on her, and she was now perplexed with what she ought to do. She realized that loving herself did not mean treating and spoiling herself with meaningless and harmful trivialities and indulging in harmful pleasures for temporary happiness. Loving herself wasn't going to be the easy vacation she imagined. If she really wanted to commit to loving herself, which she had craved for a long time, she would have to suffer and give up cigarettes. She wanted to go on a trip and give in to all her bad habits and hoped to be in love with herself after drinking and smoking for a month. I had a feeling she would love herself more if she overcame a bad habit than giving in to one.

Previously, she really didn't love herself because of her actions. She wanted to love herself before she actually knew what it meant. Once she knew what it meant, she clarified her thoughts. She said she "wanted to want" to love herself. I told her that sounded like a nice way to say she had good intentions but did not physically want to sacrifice for something worthwhile.

Sometimes we have corrupted our natural desires so that we cling to that which is detrimental and not beneficial. Under such circumstances, we might not want to love ourselves, but we always have the option to do so. I do believe that if we choose to better ourselves long enough, our body will correct its iniquities over time and then we will feel love for ourselves. Only when we take loving actions towards ourselves, then can we actually feel love for ourselves. To love herself, she would have to do what she did not want to do.

Yet, too many of us choose to wait till our wants and desires are in line with our actions. Sadly, the wise know that will not come quick enough and therefore do not wait for their desires to chase what is meaningful.

HATE

We do not know love because we do not know hate.

The dogmatic church teaching to never hate is contrary to the idea of rationally pursuing our ideals. How is this ideal? How is this righteous? We should have a natural reaction to avoid that which is bad and should react when the natural reaction is accurately identifying evil.

"But [Jesus] turned and said to Peter, 'Get behind me, Satan!
You are a hindrance to me. For you are not setting your mind
on the things of God, but on the things of man.'"
- Matthew 16:23

What is your definition of hate? We pretend that we are virtuous because we claim we do not hate despite the fact that we do it. Is hate simply being angry at somebody else? If so, then Jesus was angry and hateful in the temple when he knocked over tables. Is hate an intense natural reaction to separate yourself from someone who is impeding your God-given purpose? Then, even Jesus was hateful when He told Peter to get behind Him. To say that hate is always immoral and love is always moral is to say that Jesus was immoral at times.

If it is good to have an overwhelming feeling of love that motivates us to cling to that which is good for our pursuits, is it not equally important and equally good to have an intense feeling of hatred that motivates us to separate from that which is bad for our pursuits? If the goal is to best pursue our purpose, then both are necessary.

Why do we say that we always need more love in this world? Why do we continually devote ourselves to certain virtues? The greater man, the virtuous man, knows when to love and when to hate. He does not love those who are evil. He only has affectionate love for those who are beneficial to his pursuits. Those who oppose his pursuits are hated and avoided while being a hindrance; when they become a trusted ally, then he loves them.

Why is it that the God of the Old Testament was a God that hated and loved and judged people based on what they did but the God of the New Testament is portrayed as a God that is only capable of love? It is not that God has changed—it is that we have changed, and we have also attempted to change God to be what we want Him to be. We so badly want simplicity that we have taken God's command to be virtuous and translated the words into a command to follow a virtue.

Many say that *agapē* is mysterious because we do not understand the type of love it is. Perhaps it is only mysterious because it does not make sense to even call it love! *Agapē* is a desire to have a proper relationship with someone who is trustworthy. It requires critical thinking and judgement—not a strict obedience to the virtue of love. But we try so hard to cram a square peg into a round hole and then dance around the reality when we cannot make it work. Maybe we should find the right piece, for the path is narrow.

Perhaps it is time we face the harsh reality that our God does not love everyone. Our God is a God who loves and hates, but He is a fair judge—He is *agapē*. Perhaps we should realize that the idea that we should *hate the sin, but love the sinner* is actually unbiblical and contradicts the teachings of God.

But we so desperately love to follow virtues without consideration for the right time. We prefer to say that "*Love is a fruit in season at all times.*"[3] We embrace such sweet words even when they directly contradict the biblical teaching that there is a season for love and a season for hate.

THE INSTINCTS OF LOVE

If one is to ignore and turn away from the natural understanding that God has given him from birth, that is his instincts, and to lack any aim at all, then your body will never allow you to feel as if it is on the path towards its goal and subsequently obtain the reward of the feeling of love. You must have a desire, and we feel love when we pursue that desire.

Loving is the process of getting to the goal, but sometimes we are not successful. We can fail and have wasted our sacrifices. We can be betrayed. Our prize could be worthless in the end. The flower can prick us. The loved one can leave us. A proper relationship has two entities who both love and are compelled to love each other.

However, the worst thing can happen when you trust someone. You open yourself up to the potential of betrayal. Lucifer betrayed God. And Lucifer is now the leader of hell. It's also what Judas did to Jesus. It's what Mara did to the Buddha. It's the Greek mythological story of Troy—to be welcomed in as guests only to steal the wife of the king. It's the kind of betrayal that leads to a deadly war. To know that we can be betrayed terrifies us, as our suffering would be wasted. It perverts the ideal path and stops us from reaching the place we desire to be in the future.

To love is to trust—both carry vulnerability. It is to aim for heaven but now risk hell.

Is that sufficient? No. Perhaps, we should consider that love may not be worth it? We must have another motivation to love, as both heaven and hell are indescribably great and terrible. If anything, most may be left in the middle of the two and without a substantial reason to pursue a grand responsibility.

Love is a dangerous beast that has great potential but can also tear us apart. It is not for all, but for those who are capable of handling it—it proves to be worthwhile.

That does not mean we affectionately love all. It means that we ought to first build ourselves up to be capable of understanding others so that we can determine if they are worthwhile, and then we shape ourselves into the person who can handle a relationship. If we pursue a worthwhile relationship when we are capable of handling it, then we maximize our chance of heaven and minimize the risk of hell.

To love is to trust, but to trust is not always to love. Trust is a much larger category that does not specify an aim. Love must contain a specific aim. For example, I can trust that someone else is truthful when they say they are against me—however, that does not result in love. Love only occurs when I believe they are aiming to contribute to my instincts and I actually trust that they are doing what they claim. This is why we love our friends—because we believe they want great things for us. And yet, the love one has for his wife is much deeper because a wife has vowed to be for her husband and only the wife has the capability to contribute to certain instincts that his male friends cannot.

We ought to love carefully, with rationality and discernment. We are designed to cling to those we *trust*. We are designed to feel the greatest feeling when we engage with the instinct that encourages us to grow, but it will only grow us if we go about it rationally. Rationality minimizes the risk of hell and furthers our opportunity for success. That makes it worthwhile.

We were designed to pursue our instincts to reproduce and aim for greatness and cling to those who will help contribute to our instincts. To be *deeply in love* is to believe that the other person is truly aiming to help in your pursuit of *all of your instincts* as best they can, and to be willing to allow them to. This is why the feeling of being in love brings such happiness—you are in the process of best pursuing your instincts and now have the advantage of another to help you. Just as you might be overjoyed when you obtain a higher position in work, we ought to be overjoyed when we find someone willing to help us obtain our truest and most innate goals.

We love so that we can best survive. We love so that we achieve the greatest success in our time on earth. We love so that we can pass on a part of ourselves to the next generation, so that we can be eternal. To love is to reach for the infinite.

EVIL & BETRAYAL

If love is the willingness to suffer for the growth of something or someone, then evil is to pervert the purpose of love—to let others suffer in vain or worse, to make their suffering their downfall. Evil is not letting their suffering allow them to grow stronger and more capable. It is allowing them to suffer, only to betray them, making their suffering meaningless.

What is the difference between a gym trainer and a Nazi guard in a concentration camp giving you work orders? Both are encouraging you to suffer and telling you that there will be negative consequences if you do not oblige. Both are setting tasks that do not create something of material value to the people doing the work. The difference lies in the purpose of suffering. The Nazi guards gave tasks and kept their prisoners malnourished. The prisoners were forced to work on things that would only further lead to more destruction of themselves and those they loved. It is evil because it is done with the purpose of making people suffer unnecessarily and without a worthwhile aim. A gym trainer trains you for your growth so that *you* are in better physical shape. Despite the fact that both may tell you to pick up a boulder and move it, only to move it back to its original place, a gym trainer can be virtuous, while the other is not.

However, good intentions alone are not enough. A gym trainer who has little knowledge of his profession may have the best intentions for you to grow and become healthier, but his lack of knowledge may lead to a long-term injury if he does not know what he is doing. Knowledge and the courage to act must be paired with good intentions in order for something to truly be good.

Rationality and the courage to act must be paired with instincts in order for something to truly be good.

We must have a proper motivation and be as rational as possible.

So, how are we to react to someone with good intentions but a lack of understanding? I would not call their actions evil. It can be characterized by ignorance and bearing a responsibility that they are not yet prepared for. That is just plain stupidity and can lead to terrible results. It is the blind leading the masses. It is walking through a forest of snakes without concern for your safety. It is ignorant bliss. It may not be evil, but it is much further from love than it is from evil.

When Jesus was crucified on the cross by Roman soldiers, He knew that the soldiers were not responsible for what they were doing. They did not have evil intentions, but were merely doing their job and executing their prisoner as ordered. The soldiers did not know that they were crucifying God. While it is not ideal to be in a place where you do not know exactly what is going on, it is forgivable if they truly did not or could not know what was happening.

"And Jesus said, 'Father, forgive them, for they know not what they do.' And they cast lots to divide his garments."
-Luke 23:34

Evil and betrayal are often the cause of unnecessary suffering. And what are we to do when we are confronted with characters who are evil and likely to betray us? Leave them. Have nothing to do with them until they have become trustworthy. But what about when it is thrust upon you like in the example of a concentration camp? Then look for ways that you can willingly embrace it so that it does help you grow. This does not mean that you embrace the whole idea or that you approve of what others are doing, merely that you are looking to make the best out of the worst of situations. Let it grow your courage, your strength, your nobility and your character as much as possible.

But that does not make it acceptable for others to put it upon you with the purpose of maliciousness. What they are doing is still evil, but you can make the best of it for yourself.

And to those with overbearing love, it is not love that you have. It is a betrayal. It does not help others if you solve all their problems. It simply coddles and stagnates them. It earns their trust and keeps them dependent on your trust but leaves them to die. It's selfish. You are not allowing others to flourish and grow. It is sad when you see a parent of a drug addict who continually provides their child means for drugs that are killing them. Is it love if gifts will be used to buy more of the poison that is harming them? Would it not be better for them to say no and only offer food instead of money?

So, does that mean that we should not put our trust in others because we know that there exists the possibility that they will betray us and make us suffer in vain? No. We should embrace them bravely when we are capable, and they are most meaningful. No coward can truly love, for one must be brave to love. One must also be capable and wise for his love to be worthwhile.

IMAGINATION

If fear is that which helps steer and motivate you towards a safe path when danger is near, imagination is the engine that keeps you going forward when you have no fears present.

But if you have no purpose or no love then nothing will motivate you. Only when you are aiming at something can you be motivated. It's like pressing on the gas pedal in a car. But if the car is not aimed at a beautiful destination, why should you even bother with the effort of pressing the gas pedal? Why should you be motivated to even try?

It may very well pull you further away from the correct path as it may bring you closer by sheer luck or misfortune, and your mind knows that. Your mind knows it is a risk to drive and expend energy without direction and will not encourage such action. We must have an ideal that we are aiming at. But sometimes, it is worthwhile to explore and drive a few miles to see something worthwhile that may give us a purpose. When we do not know where to go, we should rely on cultural or traditional norms that have told us to drive in a certain direction. This can reduce the risk of going in the wrong direction by seeing other people succeed and heading in a similar direction. Perhaps that will give you the motivation to move in a direction until you see something, and then you can use your own conscience and look clearly at your desire. That is it. Follow wise guidance when you are incapable of properly guiding yourself, but when you can use your conscience to determine what is right and what is ideal, chase what you find to be ideal. That is Christianity. That is proper philosophy. (This idea will be fully explained in the chapter regarding the virtue of transcending).

It is only when we are idle, when we are bored, that we tend to ponder evil ideas. In an attempt to rid the world of evil, we have philosophies and religions to help keep us moving in a general virtuous direction. It is good to have culture telling us to do great things and pursue meaningfulness and shows us examples of greatness that we can emulate. Along the way, we should open our eyes and find the most worthwhile path that each one of us can embark upon and pursue a meaningful cause.

Like the energy that fuels our transportation, our motivation also runs out eventually. We must refuel with the imagination of the achievements of our future desire. To not have a deeply ingrained desire will result in you lacking the fuel of life to push on. Albert Einstein, Charles Spurgeon, J. Benson Hamilton and many others have all used a similar simile: *Life is like riding a bike, to keep your balance, you must keep moving forward.*[4]

The simile applies so well to the concept of love. Sometimes, things may knock you off your bike and you may get scraped, bruised or torn apart. But to stay down and avoid the possibility of betrayal ever again is to not live. It is to avoid the joys of life so that you can avoid disasters. And I understand why some may want to stay down. Disasters are capable of harming or destroying you, so baby steps are needed in that direction. Sometimes, you need to learn to walk again, and the next time, you learn to do it properly. Learn to be aware of the things that may detract you from your goal of staying on the bike.

Wisdom is not measured by the amount of knowledge you are sitting on; it is measured by your speed and direction. The same goes for love.

We must have our desires in our thoughts. We must imagine the potential that we hope to achieve and let that flame the fire and keep us marching onward.

Love is an essential virtue to fully experience humanity. But love is not all that we need! No! We need anger, forgiveness, bitterness, strength, kindness, hate, courage, honesty and love! Love is one of the many virtues we are granted, and we should utilize it at the proper time, just as all the others.

CHAPTER 6

"Consciousness is only possible through change;
change is not possible save through movement."
- Théodule Ribot[1]

Aware of a Purpose

Consciousness

It is consciousness that is uniquely visible in the lives of men of high character. They seek meaning in everything they do because they are conscious. They are always prepared and always concerned and capable of handling threats. They have their eyes open and know how to properly respond to a threat or a potential threat. When things go bad, they are prepared.

Consciousness is the state of being aware of and responsive to one's surroundings.

Consciousness can be increased or reduced. For example, the consumption of alcohol reduces consciousness, and our consciousness increases when we encounter things that are stimulating. We have consciousness for the purpose of achieving our desires, for our consciousness peaks when we are engaging with something that is on the path towards our desires, whether or not that thing is helpful.

Like all virtues, there are times when we should be conscious and times when we do not need to exert the energy that consciousness demands. While consciousness may not be ideal all the time, such as sleeping and relaxing, we should always aim to be capable of it.

We should always be capable of exerting our ability to interact and respond.

Energy of Consciousness

When I was in Utah, I went for a run to the top of a mountain in the Wasatch Range. It was a beautiful day, and I was jogging up the mountain at a good pace. Over halfway up, I became tired, but I pushed ahead in an exhausted state. The trail was narrow, winding and with bushes closing in on both sides. At one point, I randomly looked down and realized that my right foot was only half a step away from a three-foot-long snake. As you have probably noticed by now, I hate snakes with a passion.

I immediately began sprinting as fast as I could. For the next half mile, I ran faster and faster up the hill as adrenaline surged through me, and I was afraid that another snake would be on the trail. I wanted nothing more than to get out of the narrow path and onto the opening where I would be better able to feel comfortable in my surroundings. When the trail finally opened up, I was astonished that I had run at such an increased pace up the mountain for so long. Had I tried to do that without seeing a snake, I would not have had the motivation or drive to push myself with such focus and ignore the fatigue from sprinting.

In grad school, one math class required a six-hour take-home test. The test was strenuous; one of the questions, in particular, required me to look in the book to find the answer. When I was studying for the test, I had a low level of focus and found myself skimming through the book, often not retaining much knowledge. But when I had an exact question to search for, combined with the urgency of the stipulated time ticking away, I was reading through the textbook at a faster rate and with more focus than I had ever had while studying. I even read sections of the book that did not pertain to the question and learned new things that I would be using for future questions. Having a precise question and desire to find it had not only motivated me to read the information with great efficiency but also with a better understanding.

I later thought about these two events and their connection with consciousness. What surprised me upon thinking about the events is that the energy and focus that I derived from the catalyst did not only pertain to the catalyst. When running, after escaping the snake, I had extra energy to run for another half mile. In the test, I was reading through sections that did not pertain to the question with much more focus than when I was studying. For some reason, being aware of something that spiked my consciousness provided the energy to achieve the immediate desire, escaping the snake or answering the question, but it also spilled over into other aspects of my life.

Consciousness not only helps us become aware of potential dangers but also allows us to react with vigor towards events, ideas or objects and move us closer to our desires. If your desire is to survive or do well on a test, and you are conscious of these problems, then your body will naturally provide you a boost of adrenaline or focus to handle the problems. Consciousness gives us the motivation to continue in the process of love towards our desire. When we are conscious, we have the energy to handle the problems life throws at us.

Therefore, aim to have a purpose. Have many purposes. When you have a goal or a purpose, your attention and consciousness are given to things that affect that goal. When things exist around you, you will see them as tools to help you achieve your desire. If you lack purpose and nothing is changing in your life, then you have no need to pay attention to anything.

We were meant to chase something. So, find something worthwhile and meaningful and pursue it.

In writing this book, I found that everything I did had a purpose; what I watched on TV, the places I went, the people I met—all of this became more interesting because I was seeing them in a way that would help contribute to my book. I enjoyed them more, and actually pursued them because they had a reason to capture my attention. Even the things I did not expect to be useful became worth watching and exploring because they had the potential to fit into my purpose.

My body was in a state of awareness as I was searching for answers. When I compare the experience of writing a book to my experience as a senior accountant at a Big 4 accounting firm, I realized that it was a struggle just to get through the day without any real purpose. As an accountant, I did not want to become a partner at the firm nor could I find the suffering of the work meaningful. I hated the work. I had no desire to be there, and my mind would drift far from the work as I wanted to work on a desire that actually motivated me.

At the accounting firm, many tried to convince themselves that they liked the job or would consume an unhealthy amount of caffeine to keep their consciousness engaged. Perhaps caffeine makes us happier because it taps into the same system that is affected by the process of pursuing or protecting something we love. However, you can only artificially stimulate yourself for so long before your body starts rejecting it because it knows you are not really on the right path of pursuing a meaningful goal.

Another example of a drug that brings consciousness is ammonia inhalants, also known as smelling salts. To revive someone from a loss of consciousness, placing a small amount of smelling salts underneath their nose allows them to breathe in the ammonia and shocks their system. It literally wakes someone up from unconsciousness. First responders have often used it to wake people who have fainted. Boxers have historically used the drug when they become dazed from being punched in the head. The drug, while harmless, is now banned in boxing because it is so effective in stimulating their senses.

Currently, non-boxing athletes use the drug to stimulate themselves before a game and get them focused, as they are legal in all other sports leagues. Former NFL players and trainers have estimated that between 70 and 80% of NFL players have used smelling salts prior to games.[2] Professional weightlifters take a whiff of the inhalant right before they walk on stage and lift in competitions. Why? Because it wakes you up and makes you hyper-alert; that alertness translates into strength and power.

Think about it...Professional athletes, who are wide awake, take something that is prescribed for people who are unconscious. Why? Because it increases the consciousness in them. It resets their whole system and puts them in a state of shock. That state of shock, or the *flight or fight* state, makes athletes perform better. It makes them faster and stronger. Increasing consciousness and coming in contact with things that give you purpose will give you more energy. And that is all athletes want—energy!

The concept of consciousness resulting in energy is included in many religions and cultures. The Chinese call it chi (*qi*), Indians call it prana, Native Americans call it the Great Spirit, the Japanese call it Ki and the list goes on. Furthermore, the idea presented in Judeo–Christian texts is that life was breathed into man for the purpose of doing the work that needs to be done.

> "…*for the Lord God had not caused it to rain on the land, and <u>there was no man to work the ground</u>, and a mist was going up from the land and was watering the whole face of the ground— <u>then the Lord God formed the man of dust from the ground and breathed into his nostrils the breath of life</u>, and the man became a living creature.*"
>
> - Genesis 2:5–7

In some religions and cultures, the physical flow of energy is said to create a healthier life, a life of happiness and satisfaction. Some do acupuncture, some martial arts and others focus on their breathing to rebalance their energy and unblock any stalled energy in the body.

Regardless of the culture, it seems that energy or a life force is essential to helping us achieve our goals and desires. The Judeo–Christian belief is that life was breathed into man so he could work. When work needs to be done, we need a spark in us that allows us to achieve what ought to be done. Hence, we have energy when we have a desire.

We first need a purpose, something we desire, and when that is combined with things that move us closer to the desire, we become conscious of those moments. The result is an increase in energy and urgency to best handle those moments.

Having a self-determined purpose creates consciousness. Fear only affects us because the thing we fear may detract us from our desire, whether that be to live or to achieve something great or whatever we may find meaningful. *Without a purpose or desire or love, we need not fear, and as a result, we need not have consciousness.*

Consciousness is vital to the handling of our responsibilities, and as such, it is imperative that we attempt to remain conscious or at least capable of consciousness when we have to take care of things we love. Therefore, let us consider the activities that people partake in that can increase or decrease our capabilities for consciousness.

Decreasing Consciousness

A close friend of mine told me about some drama that had occurred in her household. My friend's roommate had been dumped by her boyfriend. Apparently, my friend's roommate had gotten drunk and doesn't remember what she did, but she woke up with hickeys on her neck and her boyfriend had not been the one to give them. He had broken up with her because she had been with another man while she was drunk.

I have debated in my head how I felt about the idea of drinking alcohol in the past, but I never took the time to try to understand what was really going on and to come to a solid conclusion on how I felt about it. So, when I heard the story of my friend's roommate, I was intrigued. The consideration of how alcohol affects a person had been sitting in a corner of my mind for too long, and I needed to dive into the reality of what was occurring and how one should regard the use of alcohol.

I began to ponder the idea of being drunk and if the person drinking is responsible for their actions and should bear the responsibility of what they do while blacked out or drunk. I don't think anyone would say my friend's roommate did not deserve her punishment, but something didn't sit right with me. I agreed that my friend's roommate had deserved her fate, yet I deeply felt that the blame was placed incorrectly in the act of cheating, particularly if she was so blacked out that she was unconscious of what she was doing.

Consciousness, by its very definition, is the state of being awake and aware of one's surroundings. Consciousness is what makes us human beings. It's what separates us from robots as we are aware of our unique thoughts, memories, feelings, sensations and environment. When we drink to the point of being blacked out, we essentially lose that consciousness. We lose who we are and what is most essential and defining about being human to some extent.

However, many choose to drink to dim their consciousness, which is an elegant way of stating that we drink to remove our awareness of our responsibilities from this world that weigh down on us. When we are conscious of the burdens in life, we are aware of our responsibilities, as they run through our subconscious continually. Even while responsibilities beckon from our subconscious, they can burden and wear us down. Drinking alcohol seems to have the effect of reducing the burden that consciousness bears on the mind.

Being sober leads to taking on the responsibility of being aware of accomplishments and shortcomings. Being blacked out leads to no responsibility or concern for your problems as you are unconscious of them. When driving a car, you must be sober because you need to be aware and alert while driving. You are not only responsible for yourself but also for everyone else on the road. Driving under the influence essentially means that you are driving without being conscious. You are driving using your muscle memory but may be unable to handle difficult situations or new situations that require a clear mind to decipher the ideal path.

Alcohol is technically a depressant. It sucks out the energy you get from being conscious and being aware of your desires and goals. However, this is also counteracted by the fact that you now have ignorant bliss, which allows you to feel some happiness.

Alcohol numbs the burden and pain of responsibility. It allows us to reduce consciousness and avoid the reality of life. To live our lives properly, we should aim to grow and do so by properly bearing the most meaningful burden we can manage and allow ourselves to be sharpened and shaped by the lessons and strains of suffering so that the next time we face difficulties, we might be more experienced, stronger, smarter and more capable. That's growth. That's growing up. That is love. That is transcending. That's facing our problems and not cowering away. Alcohol numbs us to our sufferings and allows us to not care about responsibilities or our fears.

And while sometimes it's beneficial and relaxing to take a break from responsibility, it is not always the right thing to do. In many difficult endeavors, it is necessary to take intermittent breaks to relax and recover because we are not prepared to accomplish the task at hand without a break. But some experiences do not allow for breaks. Some experiences require us to prepare ourselves in advance so that we can hold a responsibility until a certain task is accomplished.

I do not want to marry someone who takes a break from the responsibility of their marital contract with me. When they say they will always love me and cherish me and be faithful to me at the altar, I want that to be true.

And maybe that's why I feel so perplexed about a person who blacks out and then unknowingly cheats. The person, when blacked out, is essentially unconscious and therefore has removed all responsibility, including the responsibility towards their relationship or the marriage. How can you be mad or surprised when they cheat?

How can you not be mad about the fact that they are willingly losing consciousness (blacked out) but only be mad that they have cheated? They failed and let you down when they blacked out or became drunk enough to no longer feel the responsibility of the marriage. The idea of a relationship or marriage inherently carries responsibility, but if you're blacked out, you no longer bear that responsibility. You are just a robot following your past programming or your inherent desires. The action of cheating is the byproduct of losing consciousness and following your primitive desires without the responsibility of any relationship contracts.

It is instinct without rationality.

Regardless of whether you make it home safely or not, we know it's wrong to be unconscious when driving a car. As part of society, we are all strongly against drunk driving. Yet, we don't feel the same way about how we operate our own lives. We black out and hope we don't wreck our lives. And when we get lucky and do not crash, we think we did nothing wrong.

If you tell your spouse that you are content with them blacking out, you are allowing them to remove the all responsibilities they bear, including the responsibility of the relationship. You are allowing them to lose who they are, but you still want them to be your significant other. Yet, most individuals do not despise blacking out or getting drunk beyond the point of losing consciousness of the relationship. It is not despised because we do not associate losing consciousness with losing responsibility for the marriage. Maybe the truth that your relationship is a responsibility ought to be taught more.

Can we drink alcohol without completely losing consciousness while keeping our responsibility for our marriage contract? Yes, we can. If the responsibility is so deeply ingrained in our consciousness, it would take an extreme amount of drunkenness or a complete black out to reduce the awareness of our responsibility to the point of vanishing or cheating.

And I do not make the claim that having a single glass of alcohol is inherently immoral or should always be regarded as a bad decision. Neither am I claiming that it is good. I merely want to focus on the effect of drinking to the point that our consciousness is significantly affected.

I believe that the decision to drink comes with the acceptance of whatever consequences arise from that decision. Furthermore, we should *consider* if the decision to drink past the responsibility of the relationship may be grounds for the dissolution of the relationship. It is a brutal idea but is worth considering. It proposes that a relationship has been compromised as soon as the drunkard has had enough alcohol to remove the drunkard's responsibility from the relationship, regardless of what actions are taken. This is like saying, "Getting behind the wheel while drunk is enough for a DUI and ought to be punished."

I am not saying that I agree with the idea or support it, but we ought to consider it.

How can you be mad at someone for doing something they have no control over? No mature person should be. When they are drunk, it's incorrect to be mad at them for cheating. It's like being mad at a robot for doing what it was programmed to do. Or to be mad at a jellyfish, which has no brain or malicious agenda, for stinging you. Or being mad at a person who has blacked out for not being a good driver. You don't get mad at their hurtful actions but at the fact that they chose to drink and drive.

Without being conscious, how can you blame their consciousness and the decisions that follow related to their responsibilities? To be mad at someone for something that they are not even aware that they are responsible for is not right, but that doesn't mean you are unjustified in being upset at the end of the day.

You can be disappointed that they did not choose to be aware of their marriage responsibilities at all times, which they should have been. They decided to lose control of their consciousness and no longer take on the responsibility that the relationship required.

So, why do we not despise this act? Why do we not teach the truth that your relationship is a responsibility? To learn this truth is to become conscious of our responsibilities. Our responsibilities often bear burdens that require suffering and discomfort.

This can be compared to someone giving you the advice of not walking down a dark alley at night.

We are forgiving to those who are ignorant of their responsibilities or what they are getting themselves into. For example, if you take a stroll down a dark alley accidentally and get mugged, people will feel bad for you because you were unaware of what was going to happen to you. But if the next day, you take a stroll down the same dark alley at the same time and the same thing happens, then it is much less understandable, and you are considered a fool and no pity is awarded to you. You ought to have learned your lesson and should have been conscious of the fact that there are certain places you should avoid and not deal with when you are unable to handle them. I am not saying that it is your fault, or that it should have happened, but the reality of the world is harsh, and you need to be aware, conscious and fearful of certain areas that are not safe.

So, to learn that you have a responsibility means that you no longer have the safety net of pity. Now, you are fully responsible and the excuse, "I did not know it would happen," is no longer valid. To learn that your relationship is a responsibility means that you no longer can make this mistake and demand pity. Some of us would rather make a mistake and use their one *get-out-of-jail-free* card.

To learn that a relationship is a responsibility and to sign up for it is to give up your *get-out-of-jail-free* card. To learn this is to gain consciousness and bear responsibility. That is why you look for a responsible spouse—you want someone who is aware of their responsibilities.

The book of Proverbs, which is full of wisdom and instruction, make it clear that fools hate wisdom and knowledge because fools want to keep the responsibility of being conscious at an arm's length. If a naive person gets hurt, they will receive pity for their actions because they were unconscious of the dangers of life. However, if a foolish person chooses to continually ignore life's lessons and keep their eyes shut while living in a dangerous world, they are blindly walking into the dangers of life. The fool would rather hope to receive pity than a lesson; in effect, putting his life at risk. That is why the Bible says that the wisdom of the Lord will result in years being added to your life (Proverbs 9:11). While it won't always guarantee safety, it will increase the chances of your safety by opening your eyes; however, it comes at the cost of bearing the responsibility of consciousness. Many fools will gladly give up safety and try to receive pity for their stupid actions from those who judge them. Just as very few want to hear that drinking to an extent is irresponsible towards their marriage, very few want their spouse to know that they are aware and continue walking down that dangerous path, for then they will feel shame for they no longer can use the excuse that they did not know what would happen.

"Be sober-minded; be watchful. Your adversary the devil prowls around like a roaring lion, seeking someone to devour."
- 1 Peter 5:8

People do not always want to bear the responsibility of being aware. If you are aware and conscious when you do something bad, you cannot say that it was a crime of passion and get an easier sentence. The conscious are responsible for their actions and are expected to have learned and gained the intelligence to understand the consequences of their actions. It is without a doubt much easier in the short term to choose to avoid consciousness, but if you choose to avoid consciousness, then no mature person will choose you as a companion.

Now, let me address the difficult question of whether or not you should divorce someone after they lose consciousness without cheating. The short answer: no. You should certainly make sure that your spouse is conscious of what they have done and why they should never do it again because they were not being responsible for your marriage. However, as they are within the covenant, it ought to be forgiven until they do something that breaks the vows. We ought to spend more time understanding the meaning of love, responsibility and what the vows mean and less time choosing the wedding venue, the size of the cake and the seating arrangements.

Are they still within the bounds of the contract? Yes, for they have not cheated; therefore, offer forgiveness. You ought to forgive your spouse as long as they do not break the contract that they vowed to follow. They may falter within the bounds of the contract, but we ought to forgive them as long as they do not break it.

So why talk about this? Because we do not ignore things that are wrong but work to make the best possible decisions in the future as a man of high character would.

If you avoid doing what is right for too long, then on an unlucky day, you might do something unforgivable. And neither person wants that.

UNCONSCIOUSNESS

To dive even deeper into the abyss of rebuttals, what if the person becomes unconscious and is in a coma or is unconscious while sleeping? Are they being irresponsible towards their marriage?

In short—no. Practically speaking, when you engage in these acts that make you become unconscious and physically subdued, for example, sleeping, then you are no longer at the risk of cheating.

Consciousness and responsibility entail aiming toward the ideal.

Likewise, when you *unwillingly* become unconscious, you are not choosing to let go of your responsibilities. They are being stripped from you, despite your attempt to do what is right.

Interestingly, we can further analyze this by approaching this theory from another angle. We should consider if someone who is drugged without their consent should be held accountable for their following actions. For example, if a malevolent character slips a date rape drug into someone's drink, then takes them home when the victim is unconscious and has their way with them, would the victim be held responsible to a spouse or significant other? No. We understand the situation and disapprove of the agent that removed the consciousness.

We despise the thing or person that strips away their consciousness. However, if a person willingly and knowingly embraces the drug that makes them unconscious, then the fault lies with the person who made the decision that leads to further bad decisions.

And some will be mad at me for saying that people should not get drunk and worry about bad things happening. I am not justifying the bad things that happen to them. But I would also think it would be wise to keep yourself protected and not allow yourself to be susceptible to those who are looking for easy targets.

LETTING GO

People are required to show proof of maturity when they enter a bar, but by the time they leave, most lack what they entered with.

Some will say, "How can you be mad at me for the stupid things I said to you when I was drunk? I was basically a child when I was drunk." Surprisingly, they are right. They lose the consciousness that matured adults have developed. They lose the ability to rationalize and make wise decisions. They are hoping you will forgive them, as they were not responsible for what they did while they were under the influence. And it's a valid argument. Often, it will win the argument because you don't have the audacity to state the obvious—the problem is that they chose to become drunk.

Most avoid the truth because that would only make them hypocrites for most people have done that same thing. So, in order to save their own reputation, the truth is avoided.

They have the option to give them no punishment at all for their misbehavior or to hold them responsible (but that means to be dissatisfied with the decision to get drunk). And honestly, how can they ask someone else not to become drunk when they do the same?

So, they avoid the truth to avoid the problem and to continue in their confused ways. A quote by Friedrich Nietzsche, who despised alcohol, comes to mind: "*The strength of a spirit should be measured according to how much of the 'truth' one could still barely endure—or to put it more clearly, to what degree one would require it to be thinned down, shrouded, sweetened, blunted, falsified.*"[3]

Many claim that drinking is fun, as it helps you to relax and let loose. Restated, it means that you lose the responsibility of caring about what others around you think of your actions. I understand. Not caring what others think of you can sometimes make life more enjoyable because you can dance like no one's watching. And maybe we should just learn from that—learn that we should dance when we are not drunk because people don't care how we dance. Think about it—if you did something truly embarrassing while you were drunk, you would still feel embarrassed the next day. But when you don't do anything truly embarrassing and dance intoxicated, you don't feel embarrassed the following day because it's not something you should be embarrassed about. Dancing is not embarrassing. Yet, for some reason, when we are sober on the dance floor, we are terrified about being embarrassed because of the way we dance. The truth is that if we do something embarrassing, we are going to know one way or the other. Maybe, we should just try to learn to not be embarrassed by things we shouldn't be embarrassed about and go out and dance. Harder said than done, but still a more proper aim.

Nietzsche, who considered alcohol and Christianity to be the "*two great European narcotics*,"[4] said that both alcohol and Christianity were being used to reduce negative feelings. And he was right. The release of sadness, discomfort and burdens are the selling points of preachers and alcohol. This is how they make their money. They tell you that you don't need to worry about a thing and put your problems elsewhere. Let your problems go because these magical powers can numb your pains. They give short-term solutions that blind you to legitimate concerns, instead of dealing with the problem and assuming proper responsibility.

And I am not saying that Christianity is everything that

Nietzsche says it is. But too often, it is used as such. Too often, I see pastors presenting sermons about letting go of your burdens and unconditionally forgiving others so you will feel better. They preach that you should have no fears and give all of your worries to God and forget about them. Yet, the Bible does not actually preach that—only some pastors do—but it sure does go down smooth, regardless of whether it is actually good for you.

SLEEP

Sleep deprivation can also put you in a state of decreased consciousness. In 2000, Dr. A. M. Williamson, a professor at the University of New South Wales, and Anne-Marie Feyer, a professor at the University of Otago, tested the cognitive and motor performance impairments in participants who were sleep deprived and intoxicated.[5] The goal was to see if the loss in consciousness from alcohol is comparable to the loss in consciousness when sleep deprived.

The study found that when a subject had a blood alcohol concentration (BAC) of 0.05%, the response speed decreased by about 8–15%, hand-eye coordination decreased by about 10% and spatial memory decreased by about 13%. At a BAC of 0.1%, which is over the legal limit for adults to drive, the "performance was poorer for all measures for all tests and some measures showed more than twice the decrement at a BAC of 0.05%."

For the sleep deprivation part of the study, the participants regularly engaged in similar tests and did not sleep for a 28-hour period. The participants were given cognitive tests throughout the sleep deprivation period.

"The results indicate that on average, [a BAC of] 0.05% equivalence occurred after being awake for around 16.91 to 18.55 hours...At a BAC of 0.1%, equivalence occurred after between 17.74 and 19.65 hours of wakefulness."

The study revealed that a lack of sleep can have effects that are comparable to what alcohol has on the body. Rest is important. It's so important and vital to our well-being and proper functioning that the tireless God even rested on the seventh day as an example for us (Genesis 2:2). We were also taught the principle of taking one day off of work per week in the Ten Commandments.

LYING

Another way to reduce our consciousness is by accepting lies told by others or by lying to ourselves. As the meaningful path requires us to be conscious of problems and our responsibilities, to have someone else lie to us would only tear us away from that path. This is same as the idea of betrayal. Being lied to by someone we trust is simply a betrayal. To be told you do not need to be conscious of something that you need to be conscious of in order to be properly situated in this life is a betrayal. For example, if someone says that you do not need to be afraid of all snakes that might result in you not being conscious of the fatalities associated with snakes. You might see a rattlesnake and bend down to pick it up, only to be bitten and injected with venom. It might be comforting to believe that you have nothing to fear, but when you realize that you were not told the truth, you will realize you were betrayed.

On the other extreme, to be told that you need to be conscious of something that you do not need to be conscious of is an equal lie of betrayal. For example, to tell someone to be afraid of things that are not dangerous or that they are capable of handling will only keep them from engaging in something that could be of great use.

INCREASING CONSCIOUSNESS BY PURPOSE

So, how are we to increase our consciousness? Or at least, how are we to increase our capability of being conscious? In order to even consider having consciousness, one must have a purpose. All of the other things that can increase or decrease consciousness depend on how conscious you are of your purpose.

For example, if you have a presentation tomorrow and desire to do well, then you have a purpose. If some breaking news comes out the night before your presentation that you must now include in your presentation, this would send your adrenaline rushing, and you would race to find a way to alter the presentation to incorporate the new information. But if you were less conscious of your purpose—say you were drunk—then you might not feel the desire to take up the task of doing the extra work.

Our desires, our purposes are goals. To aim at that goal is to take up responsibility and say, "I have a desire to achieve this, and I am willing to sacrifice for it." That's a responsibility. And to drink or to reduce our consciousness only serves to reduce our responsibility and care for anything that may affect the outcome of the thing we cherish.

MEANINGFUL PURPOSE

To increase your level of consciousness, you must first begin by choosing a purpose that means something to you. The more meaningful the endeavor you are pursuing, the more conscious of it you will be. How truly devoted will you be to something if you know your efforts and your sacrifices will be better put to use elsewhere?

When I drive through the mountains, I have a strange desire to run to the top of the mountains that pass me by. I don't need a race, a crowd at the top, a photo to share on social media or a prize. I just want to do it for the pleasure I imagine I would get running up. I always thought this was strange. I thought it was meaningless.

But that isn't true. To climb a mountain gives you the reward of accomplishment. It develops your muscles and trains your cardiovascular system. To have a dream and to accomplish a difficult task is meaningful as it imbibes a work ethic within you. That work ethic will translate to other fields. Furthermore, being in nature seems to reset those who do not often have the experience of being in nature every day.

But I can't do it every day, for other things are also meaningful, like providing for a family. Running to the top of the mountain doesn't usually pay bills. It may not be the most meaningful thing to do every day, but it may be the most meaningful thing I can do occasionally. You have to create a hierarchy of what is most meaningful, and sometimes the hierarchy changes based on the time and when certain areas are lacking attention. If you work half the day, then for the second half of the day, the most meaningful thing should not be to make money anymore, but what is next on the hierarchy. It's like accomplishing a desire and moving on to the next.

So, set out for what is most meaningful. Put your desires in a hierarchy of most important and meaningful to the least. Focus on the things that are at the top of the list and imagine them coming to fruition. Visualize them. Let them inspire you. Let them grow you. Realize that if you do not move along the path towards your goal, you will become overwhelmed with less meaningful responsibilities.

I believe that we find what is meaningful when we rationally pursue our instincts. Not habits, but the instincts you were born with. When we rationally aim to better ourselves, to reproduce, to survive, then we are pursuing the path that God instilled in us from birth. The rational pursuit of such things brings about the greatest levels of joy.

We can all find people who are so burdened with mediocre responsibilities that they get stuck with them for the rest of their lives because they pursued things that did not grow them but left them in a worse place than before. Let them be an example of what may happen to you if you do not pursue what is meaningful with urgency. The truth is that sometimes we can potentially get to such a low place that we cannot recover. I beg you to never get to that point, for it can be impossible to escape. Go with passion, chase what you ought to. Strive for greatness towards your meaningful desires and passions and follow love.

> "If we decide to leave the riddles unanswered, that is a choice; if we waver in our answer, that, too, is a choice: but whatever choice we make, we make at our peril... Each must act as he thinks best; and if he is wrong, so much the worse for him. We stand on a mountain pass in the midst of whirling snow and blinding mist, through which we get glimpses now and then of paths which may be deceptive. If we stand still, we shall be frozen to death. If we take the wrong road, we shall be dashed to pieces. We do not certainly know whether there is any right one. What must we do? 'Be strong and of a good courage.' Act for the best, hope for the best, and take what comes... If death ends all, we cannot meet death better."
> - James Fitzjames Stephens[6]

Do we look at life this way? Do you see yourself at the top of a frigid mountain trying desperately to get warm? Or do you see yourself sitting in your comfortable bed, scrolling through devices waiting for the next moment of fleeting happiness? We don't see the reason for courage when we have a comfortable life. Why risk moving when we are already safe? We are warm and don't have to worry about freezing to death in the coming moments if we stand still.

So, we sit. Wrapped in warmth. All the comforts of life at our feet. We are not in chaos. We are in perfect order. Or so it seems. Until we realize we have all grown fat, have no strength and are dying from health problems because we have neglected exercise.

Some love their safety so much that they cannot bear moving away from it. They see no point in taking risks. They see no point in transcending and becoming great.

We have secured our safety and physiological needs (water, air, food)—the lowest of needs according to Maslow's hierarchy of needs. But are we willing to give up the good things to go for the great? Are you willing to risk your safety to achieve the magnificent? Because if you don't, you will eventually lose the good anyway. It seems to me that we are being told more and more that we are just fine the way we are.

We distort the definition of words just to make us feel happy and avoid reality. For example, our society has begun to idealize plus-sized models to the point where a model can be valued and glorified without accounting for unhealthy behaviors. Have we forgotten that a model is meant to serve as something we want to emulate? A *role model* is someone who exhibits ideal behaviors and characteristics that we should look up to and imitate. A model ought to be the same. But instead of looking up to models and striving to be like them, we have become lazy, lowered our standards instead of rising to reach them and have redefined the meaning of a model to fit our happiness. Or we say, "Oh, some of them are too skinny, so now we need to balance it by adding in those who are fat." As if adding another imperfect model makes up for it. Oh, what a pathetic generation we are. Don't be like them. Aim for the perfect. Aim for sanctification. Aim for the standards you would impose upon someone that you love and want to see grow. Have an ideal you aim at and make that your desire.

Or shall we kill the ideal? Shall we be like Cain and kill our brother who is able and whose sacrifice and sufferings have pleased the ultimate judge? Shall we kill the ideal so we don't have to cope with the fact that we fall short? Or shall we listen? And change and become better and more like the ideal?

Some may respond with "Who are you to judge?" when you tell them what you think is ideal. And I will respond by saying that I am a man made in the image of God. And God is the ultimate judge. That does not make me the ultimate judge, but it does make me, to some degree, capable of judging and determining what I believe the ideal to be.

Judging is necessary if you want to live a great life and want to aim for something great. To tell someone not to judge is like telling them to not strive for greatness. So, have an ideal and judge other options accordingly. And if others are offended that you judge, then ask them: Who are you to judge me for judging?

Determine what is most meaningful in your life and chase it. Emulate the great and do not stoop to the low standards of those who lower their own standards. The truth is, regardless of the level of comfort or the weather, if you stand still for too long, you will deteriorate. But if you move, if you chase something beautiful, if you have the courage and daringly embrace a novel desire, you may thrive. Only when you move, do you have the potential to be admired and respected, and people will look up to you. And it's not that you should seek and depend on the admiration of others, but we humans innately know what ought to be respected. Consciousness is something that often earns admiration. It grows an individual and society, and it creates a better place for all. That is why it is noble and admired.

We have destroyed the ideal. We have killed the idea that there is an ideal type of man that we should strive to be. We have lowered our standards so much that our standards accept everyone. This is not how we should behave. We should say, "This is what I find beautiful, and this is what I am pursuing for this is the best example of a great person." What else is the model you choose, other than a representation of the pinnacle of your philosophy?

What concerns me most is how the general population has

accepted the notion that we should not have an ideal. Before, if someone spoke a truth that was mean, the world would say that the truth was more important than hurt feelings. But, now, people cry and reject any logic if you make the same argument. Are we becoming more naive and more sensitive? Or are we just giving a larger platform and voice to the immature and those unable to cope with the truth for the first time through social media? The young are now overwhelmingly listening to the immature, who are captivating them with comedy and then sharing their uneducated opinion. The young ought to have the right to do so, but they do so at the risk of being misinformed.

In return, we can combat this by also speaking up, for the same platforms have been granted to the rest of us. We need to say that this is nonsense. We need to grow up and become capable of dealing with the truth, to realize that things are scary in this world, and we should be afraid too. Do not lie to yourself just for the sake of blissful ignorance. Grow up and aim to be virtuous, not cowardly and incapable of something great. Do not cling to your safety—your happy feelings—at the cost of pursuing what is meaningful.

THE VENTURE

In conclusion, we are conscious of things that affect our desires. Desires carry responsibilities. A man of high character is willing and capable of putting in the work to have something beautiful emerge in the end. A man of high character is willing to wrestle with the worthwhile and experience change; as a result, he will obtain a heightened level of consciousness.

The weaker man is overcome by the burden of responsibilities. Sometimes, it's easier to believe that we should just be blissfully ignorant and ignore the snakes. That we should drink our problems away. It's not exactly drinking to get rid of our desires or responsibilities but to not have to deal with the burden that the responsibility comes with that may lead you to never reach your desire.

So, if you want to partake in the heroic path that a man of high character dares tread, you should search for worthwhile responsibilities. Desire something beautiful that changes you and helps you or the community you are in grow.

You can be blissfully ignorant or be conscious and bear the responsibilities of being aware and dealing with dangers. The choice is yours and, make no mistake, you *are* making a choice. So, you can decide to stay still or venture towards something meaningful with your eyes wide open.

CHAPTER 7

*"How often must I tell you that we are made wise not by
the recollections of our past, but by the responsibilities of our
future?"*
- George Bernard Shaw[1]

Lifeguard on Duty

Responsibility

When should you bear a meaningful responsibility? When Jesus took
my sin upon His shoulders it was a beautiful act of sacrifice. His death
paid the debt I owed and allowed me to be reconciled to God. While
Jesus's sacrifice can pay for everyone's sin, not everyone receives this
gift. Some might ask, "Why doesn't Jesus save everyone?" Answer:
because he is a man of high character.

Taking on responsibility is sometimes the proper and virtuous
thing to do but not all the time. Therefore, to bear responsibility is
neither always good nor always bad. We need to understand when it
is proper to take on responsibilities.

Permission

The first prerequisite to taking on responsibility is to be given
permission to bear that responsibility. Let's see an example. Say you
are walking up stairs and an elderly woman near you is having trouble
getting to the top. Being the gentleman that you are, you stick out
your arm to offer help. Most likely, the woman will reach her arm
towards your outstretched arm, and you will help her on her journey.

At the top of the stairs, she will most likely be grateful for your help.

Now, let's change the actions slightly. You decide that you want to be more responsible and bear the heaviest burden around you. You want to eliminate the suffering and discomfort that other people endure, so you choose to help someone going up stairs. You see the first person walking up, and you run up behind them and pick them up and start carrying them up each step. When you finally get to the top, the person looks at you like you are crazy and angrily asks why you carried them up the stairs. Even if you explain your intentions, however pure they were, the person you carried will not be grateful. If you are unlucky, you might even face negative consequences for your actions.

These two scenarios highlight the idea that you must be granted permission to bear the responsibility for someone else before bearing their responsibility. To take responsibility for someone else's burdens without permission is wrong. It is taking away their freedom to be able to bear the responsibility themselves.

You would not go into a gym and lift weights for other people when they are trying to work out. They are there to suffer and work their muscle fibers so that they can tear and grow back stronger and bigger to handle the weight better next time. However, if you are there and are lightening the load, you are depriving them of the opportunity to work their muscles.

Not only would it take away their option to bear responsibilities and engage in the heroic path, but you are controlling their life without their express permission. You might think you know the right answer or what is best for others, but it is not your place to make decisions for other people unless they grant you permission.

This is no trivial matter. The thought that some know better than others and should have the right to bear another's responsibility can lead to tyrannical governments that strip you of the ability to be virtuous. When we preach responsibility, we must go about it properly and not blindly grasping at any responsibility we can hold on to.

There are some exceptions to this prerequisite of permission, the main example being those who are unable to be responsible for themselves (children), in which case the child's guardians are responsible. Another example would be Good Samaritan laws, which allow legal protection to a person who provides reasonable assistance to someone who is incapacitated or in serious peril or chaos.[2]

CAPABLE

We consider minors, those being under the age of 18, as a population that automatically gives their parents permission for their responsibility because the minors are often incapable of handling responsibilities properly. In this case, guardians have the assumed permission of being responsible for their dependents until they reach the age of 18.

Another example of someone who is incapable of having responsibility is someone who is intoxicated. If it is found that the person was not in the proper state of mind, a contract made under such circumstances is considered void and not required to be upheld.

Everyone over the age of 18, who is in a proper state of mind, is assumed to be capable of being responsible for themselves and are given the freedom to do as they please.

However, just because you are considered old enough to take on responsibility does not mean you always should. Before taking on responsibilities for other people or for yourself, make sure you are reasonably capable of accomplishing the task or at least are being truthful with the person you are bearing the burden for.

Marriage, like many great responsibilities, may be too overwhelming for some who are unable to handle it and may result in stagnation in all other aspects of one's life. It is best to operate in an environment where responsibility is challenging but where you can also take a moment to rest and reflect and see where you can improve your general circumstances.

For example, if you open a restaurant and work every hour of every day and just keep working away, you will feel stagnated. Try to get to a place where you can work and also take time off periodically to think about a new menu or how to alter or improve the atmosphere and bring excitement to the establishment. Take some time to dive into the chaos that might have worthwhile returns. Such things are what we live for.

In the same way, do not get married if that means you will have to give up everything in your life just to sustain the marriage. Hence, the idea that you should have something going or gain some value or capability before you bear the enormous responsibility of marriage so that you can properly bear it and come out stronger.

There are even circumstances where you don't need to be capable of accomplishing the task today. If it is worthwhile to fail and gain valuable experience so that it can be applied to future successful endeavors, then consider it in your capability.

RESPONSIBILITY OF JESUS

Before we get further into the idea of responsibility, I would like to start with an example so that we can understand what I am referring to when I mean responsibility. The biblical story of Jesus Christ is the perfect example of a man taking on responsibilities, which is why the West, which has generally adopted Christian teachings, emphasizes responsibility.

To understand the story of Jesus, you have to understand some of the basic precepts of Christianity. In order to get to heaven, according to Christianity, one must be sinless before God. However, as all of us have sinned, we need God to forgive our sins so that we can enter heaven. In order to pay for your sins, a sacrifice equal in value must be made to pay for your sins. Prior to the year 70 AD[3], Jews would sacrifice animals at an altar to pay for their sins. God required that the animals must have no blemishes and ought to be spotless; in other words, the sacrifice must be the best possible sacrifice to pay for your sin, as the cost of the sin is much more than any animal's worth.

Yet, none of the animals sacrificed were truly capable of covering the cost of each person's sins. The sacrifices served as a symbol for the future sacrifice to come. The sacrifice to come had to be a human who was perfect in all senses. That sacrifice was Jesus. He was the man born to die. He was sinless as a child and adult, and therefore, he was *capable* of bearing the responsibility of reconciling humanity to God.

However, even after Jesus died on the cross, many people on earth were still destined for hell. There is another prerequisite that Jesus needed to observe in order to bear the responsibility for each person. Each person has to be willing to give *permission* to Jesus to take on the responsibility and cleanse them of their sins.

For you can try to do it yourself, but you will be unsuccessful. You are like the old lady who is unable to walk up the stairs, and Jesus is the gentleman with His hand outstretched to each person offering to help them up. He is not going to pick up each person and carry them to the top without their permission. He respects their freedom and, therefore, is waiting for His followers to accept him as the savior before He can take on responsibility for their shortcomings. In other words, He wants you to give Him permission to help you get to the top.

Therefore, He took on responsibility properly, but what makes this story so interesting is the type of responsibility He took on. In Fyodor Dostoyevsky's *The Brothers Karamazov*, one character says, "*Every one is really responsible to all men for all men and for everything.*"[4] When I first heard this, I thought as many have and shrugged it off because the idea seems impossible and impractical. The character doesn't know how to explain it either, saying "*I don't know how to explain it to you, but I feel it is so, painfully even.*"[5] How could he explain it? For you are not responsible for my sins, nor should you be held accountable for them. I think Dostoyevsky's character knew that the ideal person could bear such a responsibility, yet none of us are him and would have trouble understanding how to apply it to our lives. For only if someone was truly a perfect human, could they be willing to bear the responsibility for everything that a person has done.

But how are we mere humans to do that? It is not possible for me to be accountable for your sins, for nothing I can do will wipe that sin away. But Jesus could be that sacrifice. He was capable of bearing the burden of everyone's sins and, therefore, bearing the responsibility for all men and for everything. That is the ultimate responsibility—to not only take on your own responsibilities but others that you love when they need and ask for it.

THE OUTCOME

Jesus took on more responsibility than any other man ever has or ever can. He was capable of bearing it and came out victorious and created a better place for all of us.

See, when we bear meaningful responsibilities properly, we personally grow, or we grow our communities and make the world a better place. If someone spends time creating new technology, then we all benefit from it. If someone creates a new medicine that saves lives, the community is safer, and our lives are better off. Only when something is forced on others, does it have the potential to eternally create a worse place, for people would no longer buy it if it was not forced upon them and they had the ability to speak freely.

Jesus took on a burden so much more meaningful than what we could do that the outcome also had to be equally as groundbreaking. He didn't just make the community a slightly better place; He gave us a place that was perfect. He prepared a place for us in heaven. The greater man, when successful, brings forth results proportionate to the amount of meaningful responsibility he properly undertakes.

The story of Jesus is that He properly bore the ultimate responsibility because He was capable and obtained permission to bear the responsibility. He then went through the ultimate suffering and bore the ultimate responsibility, thereby creating a place that was ultimately great. That is why a place in heaven was prepared for us after Jesus came to earth and died. Because Jesus was the ultimate example of the ideal, and the gift of heaven was the ultimate reward.

Jesus was sent to earth to be an example of the ideal man. Don't get me wrong, I know the Bible says He was sent here to save us but isn't that what the ideal man would do regardless? The greater man is on a mission to live righteously and promote and further that which he loves. Otherwise, couldn't God have just forgiven everyone who believes in Him and shown mercy for their sins? God could have, but He also wanted us to know how to live properly so He gave us an example. He gave us a man of high character.

A man of high character engages with the most worthwhile responsibilities he can bear. He consciously aims to maximize his usefulness in areas that he is allowed and to exert his capabilities towards meaningful causes over his lifetime.

WHY PURPOSE AND RESPONSIBILITY?

We need a purpose. We need a challenge. We need something that justifies the suffering, discomfort and tragedies we face. The idea that one needs to have a purpose and pursue in order to create something meaningful and worthwhile such that it outweighs their suffering has been around for a while. Viktor Frankl, a psychiatrist who survived the Holocaust, conceptualized logotherapy in his book *Man's Search for Meaning*.[6] Logotherapy helped people focus on finding a purpose in their life as a method of therapy. He developed the idea as a result of spending grueling years as a prisoner in Nazi concentration camps, where he observed that those who had a purpose and a desire in their life had a chance of surviving, and soon after someone gave up on all their desires and purposes, their body withered away. Obviously, having a purpose did not save everyone, but it became clear to Frankl that if you did not have a purpose that inspired you to live or that made life worth living, then your body and mind surely deteriorated.

You are alive. And if you want to stay that way, find a purpose. Have many purposes if you can bear them properly. Have the desire to love, to create, to help, to restructure the weak establishments within yourself.

There are many great places, accomplishments and things to experience in this world, and I hope you conquer them all. But even more importantly, I hope you always have something worthwhile and great you are striving after that truly invigorates and inspires you to live life to the fullest. If not, then I hope that you search for what does.

BECOMING A MAN

A boy becomes a man when he begins bearing his own responsibilities. Philosophers have mentioned that in order for a child to become a man, he must no longer rely on his father. The reason is that when the father is gone, there is no authority making decisions for you. There is no one controlling you. Alone you are completely battling chaos because you are out of someone else's control and must face problems and bear burdens that may allow you to grow.

It is the moment that you choose to no longer follow orders from others, but instead decide to be an individual and think for yourself.

You obviously should consider others' opinions, but you need to actually use the God-given conscience that you were destined to use and think for yourself when you are capable.

To grow up and become a man is to say "*I will face chaos because I am no longer under the protection of the structure set up before me.*" You walk toward chaos and willingly face it when you believe it is worthwhile and may lead to growth. Men need the freedom to choose—freedom to be responsible for their actions. They need to earn the acclaim, significance and respect among others so that they have value.

Separate yourself from your father's strict guidance and go out into the unknown when you are capable of handling it. Fight your own battles and learn to deal with problems using your own abilities and understanding. Yes, retain the valid principles that you were taught, but think for yourself about what is the ideal.

A good father doesn't have to die or become physically separated from his children to help them grow. A good father has to be willing to allow his children to face chaos when they are capable of handling it and when it is good for them—to allow them to face the unknown and possible death to pursue something meaningful. That's why God allowed His son Jesus to die for us. That's why Abraham took his son to the altar and was prepared to sacrifice him. They allowed their sons to face death and suffering because what the children would be doing was meaningful in their eyes. They believed God's will was more important than safety or comfort.

Maybe, the lesson we ought to learn from these stories is that happy and healthy is not the only thing we should desire for our children. A meaningful life full of sacrifice, persistence and virtuousness in the face of fear or tranquility is what we should desire and instill in our children.

Yin–Yang

If we can briefly talk about the concept of yin–yang, it might help understand how to properly take on responsibility and why Jesus was baptized.

Yin–yang is the image of a circle with a white side and a black side with one opposite-colored dot inside each side. Yin and yang come from a Chinese philosophy that shows how two contrary entities can be complementary and can be literally translated as dark and bright.

Yin–yang represents the idea of incorporating some order and some chaos in your life. You do not want too much chaos, or you will find yourself overwhelmed with the unknown, the dangerous world, and will not be able to cope with your surroundings properly. If you have too much order, then you will get bored and feel stagnant and slowly decline as your conscience becomes unused and your humanity deteriorates. Under this philosophy, the ideal path is to engage in both aspects of light and dark, or the order and chaos, so that they can work together to create something new.

The number of unknowns that you tackle should be in direct proportion to the amount of structure you have set up under you. Just as a CEO of a large company takes on an extremely chaotic role, he or she also has a lot of experience (order and structure) to deal with the large amount of chaos that may come with the role.

Imagine you have a seed that you want to grow into a tree. If you have only soil, then your seed will wither and never grow. If you have no soil and only water, then you will drown the seed in water, and it will not grow for its roots will have nothing to attach to. If you add the proper amount of water to the soil, then the seed may grow. Therefore, just as we must have the proper amount of water to make a plant grow, we need a proper amount of chaos in our lives. *Water has always been a representation of chaos.* Land is the representation of order and structure. Combined in the right amount, they create growth.

CREATION

Now, let us understand how the Bible talks about water. At the beginning of the Bible, God creates the earth and He saw that it "*was formless and empty, darkness was over the surface of the deep, and the Spirit of God was hovering over the waters.*"(Genesis 1:2). How can it be formless and empty but also full of water for isn't water substance? The answer is that the words "*formless and empty*" in Hebrew do not mean void of everything. It had a different meaning in Hebrew that the ancient readers could actually understand and relate to.

In the context of Genesis 1:2, water literally means water. The Hebrew word for empty (wā·bō·hū) means "vacuity," which is a state of *lack of thought or intelligence; empty-headedness.*" The Hebrew words for *formless* and *the deep* (tō·hū and tə·hō·wm) are both the Hebrew conative words of *Tiamat*, the Babylonian goddess of chaos.[7] Understanding the story of Tiamat will help shed some light on what the creation story in the Bible is actually portraying.

The ancient Jews were familiar with the mythology of Babylon, just as we might know of the stories of the Greek gods like Hercules and Zeus.[8] The reference to *Tiamat* was to refer to the very essence of the character, which was chaos. In other words, the verse means that the world was lacking in intelligence and was like *Tiamat (chaotic),* and the Spirit of God was over the water. But who is *Tiamat*?

Tiamat was the Goddess of Chaos who represented the saltwater in the ancient primordial Babylonian creation myth called the *Enuma Elish*.[9] When Tiamat's husband, who was the personification of order, was slain, she became frantic, plotted evil and waged war on her offspring.

A god named Marduk volunteered to fight Tiamat under the condition that he would be crowned the exalted king if he prevailed. As the only god willing and capable to fight Tiamat, Tiamat's offspring accepted his terms, and Marduk went to battle with Tiamat. Marduk defeated the goddess and took her body, which represented chaos, and ripped it in half and created the heavens and the earth with each half of the body. Marduk then took the *Tablet of Destines* from the enemy and became the possessor of destiny. He was crowned the "Victorious King" and was celebrated as a worthy leader over other gods.

The main idea of the Babylonian myth is that there was a water goddess who represented chaos, and she was killed by a brave warrior who then took the defeated chaos and created something beautiful from it.

Looking back at the biblical creation account, which was written down hundreds of years after the Babylonian creation myth was written, it makes sense to look at the words *"formless"* and *"deep,"* which are derived from the name of Tiamat, as chaotic waters. It would then read, "*the world was water, which was chaotic, and without conscious thought.*"

Where there was only chaotic water, God added in light, sky, land, plants, stars and animals; each time He created something new, He said it was good. God saw the chaos and chose to make order out of it.

Why is it important to know all this? Because it shows that the authors of the Bible knew that bodies of water were the representation of chaos. This is why Noah, who followed God's orders, survived the chaos that wiped out everyone else through the flood. This is why Moses parted the Red Sea and walked through it with thousands of believers but which swallowed those who did not obey God. This is why Jesus walked on raging waters in a storm and then calmed it because He was in control of everything, including the chaotic waters. In Revelation, John tells us that the Beast will emerge from the sea at the end of times (Rev. 13), and when he speaks of heaven, he says there will be no sea (Rev. 21:1), meaning that there will be no chaos.

The idea of wrestling with chaos and creating something great out of it is a fundamental idea in the Bible. That is why the story of creation is the first story of the Bible. It is also the first story that we are told of the adult version of Jesus in the Bible.

BAPTISM

The story of Jesus's baptism begins with John the Baptist in the rivers beyond the town of Jordan, who was baptizing people so that they would repent and turn away from their wrongful ways. While John could not save them from their sins, he wanted to prepare them to be on the right path so that when their savior would come, they would be prepared.[10]

While John was baptizing people, Jesus walked up to him and asked to be baptized. John was puzzled. He tried to deter Jesus and said, "*I need to be baptized by you, and do you come to me?*"[11] John the Baptist had been baptizing people so that they would turn from their wrong ways. Yet, Jesus was requesting to be baptized, which puzzled John because Jesus was perfect and therefore did not have wrong ways to turn from.

But Jesus wanted to be baptized for a different purpose. Yes, God had commanded Him, but God tends to make commands only when they are meaningful. And this was extremely meaningful. Jesus responded, "*It is proper for us to do this to fulfill all righteousness*,"[12] and so John baptized Him.

In both Greek and Hebrew, the word baptism means to "*be immersed*," and Jesus wanted to be fully immersed in water—*the representation of chaos.* Jesus is like the strong Marduk, willing to face chaos because, in doing so, He would create order and a better world. He is like the soil and the seed, ready to take on water so that growth may occur. Therefore, he immersed Himself in it. He was strong enough to bear the weight of chaos. He went to John because John was a devout believer and was there to support Him and help bring Him out of the water if Jesus needed it. I don't think Jesus needed the help, but this shows the idea that we should have trustworthy friends around to help us deal with chaos.

After being immersed in chaos, we expect to see growth if we have enough capabilities to handle the chaos. And Jesus, being the perfect man, obviously was prepared to handle it. And what is the result of taking on meaningful chaos that you can handle? You emerge from the chaos stronger. Then Jesus emerged from the water, the heavens opened up and God said, "*This is my son with whom I am well pleased.*"[13]

He is the man who will continually face chaos. He then walked in the desert for 40 days while being tempted by the devil. He was nailed to a cross and tortured. And yet, He conquered it all. And as a reward, He was crowned the King of Kings. His battle with chaos led to a great destiny for not only himself but all men under the New Covenant.

Isn't that the story of the Bible? We have chaos, and we have a man of high character. The man aims for something great and is willing to face the chaos. The man of high character properly handles the chaos and creates something new and beautiful. He is brutally tortured, hung on a cross and crucified for a meaningful cause and brings forth a new covenant that can reconcile humans to God.

So, what is baptism? Baptism is the declaration that you accept Jesus's teachings and are, therefore, willing to wrestle chaos for as long as it takes to obtain the worthwhile transcendence that comes from the struggle. It is to show your devotion to embarking on the virtuous path.

It is to be willing to walk into the unknown when you are capable of bearing the burden. It is to dare to learn about that which you do not know but you believe will be useful. It is to take a risk that you expect to pay out. It is to tear your own muscles for the purpose of growth. It is to suffer for the betterment of yourself and those that you love. It is to get off the couch and dare to live your life to its full extent.

It's the same story as Noah and the flood. A man heard God's instructions and followed the directions given to him to build a boat. Then, water consumed the entire earth, and only the man who was righteous and had followed God's instructions, thus preparing for the chaos, lived to make a better new world after emerging from the chaos.

"...when God's patience waited in the days of Noah, while the
ark was being prepared, in which a few, that is, eight persons,
were brought safely through water. Baptism, which corresponds
to this, now saves you, not as a removal of dirt from the body
but as an appeal to God for a good conscience, through the
resurrection of Jesus Christ..."
- 1 Peter 3:20–21

It's the idea that you should face the chaos so that something beautiful comes about as a result. And what do both stories have in common at the end? A dove. A dove is the symbol of the Holy Spirit.[14] It is the symbol of the transcendent. (See the next chapter for further explanation.)

It is the biblical story of David versus Goliath. An army stood before a giant adversary and all were too scared to face Goliath in battle. Then, a young man named David who had spent his time wrestling lions and building up his capabilities is introduced. David believed that he was capable and volunteered to face the giant. He used his cunningness to defeat the terrifying adversary and was then praised by his people and later made king by God as God declared David to be a man on the right path. He is the type of man we should inspire to be.

> "*Then they asked for a king, and God gave them Saul the son of Kish, a man of the tribe of Benjamin, for forty years. And when he had removed him, he raised up David to be their king, of whom he testified and said, 'I have found in David the son of Jesse a man after my heart, who will do all my will.'*"
> - Acts 13:21–22

Perhaps, we will never know why we are here, but we know what is pleasing to God. And for some strange reason, it is pleasing to us as well. When we properly pursue our instincts to survive and grow and create a better world, bear those responsibilities and accomplish them, we gain a feeling of satisfaction and purpose. It is as if we were created to bear responsibility. We may never know why, but it is right to struggle with a meaningful responsibility to create something beautiful.

> "*And God said, 'Let there be light,' and there was light. And God saw that the light was good.*"
> - Genesis 1:3–4

In life, we should aim to attain the maximum amount of greatness. But how can we reach so high without setting our roots as deep? We must dig deep by bearing maximum responsibility and meaningful suffering so that we can reach greatness.

THE GREAT RESPONSIBILITY

What is the greatest responsibility we can pursue?

To have *agapē* for God and everyone. Or as I would put it, to desire to have a proper relationship with God and with everyone. These two commandments, according to Jesus, are the greatest commandments of all. These are the ideas that all biblical laws and principles were built on.

The statement makes sense when we apply the concept to our neighbors and acquaintances. But what about God? How do you have *agapē* for God? Well, God is perfect, so I can assume He meets your standards. Therefore, pursue a relationship with God as well.

Question: How do you pursue a relationship with God? *Answer:* By meeting His standards. *Question:* How do you receive forgiveness for all your sins so that you meet God's standard of perfection? *Answer:* Follow and believe Jesus's teachings and devote yourself to always pursuing His teachings.

"For this is the agapē of God, that we keep his commandments."
- 1 John 5:3

"But whoever keeps his word, in him truly the agapē of God is perfected. By this we may know that we are in him."
- 1 John 2:5

You may be wondering how I could ask you to *be a man and think for yourself* and to *follow Jesus's teachings* all at once. How can we do both?

We can do both because Jesus taught us to think for ourselves. The underlying theme of Jesus's teachings were to think about what is the right thing to do and do it. He did not want us to blindly follow rules, but to be righteous and virtuous. He did not ask us to always forgive but to forgive in a virtuous manner (as God does). Not to always love others romantically or like a brother but to have love for those who are deserving of your love (to have *agapē* as God does). Not to marry someone blindly but to marry the right person at the right time. To not always fear but fear when it was appropriate. To not always bear another's responsibility but to become capable of bearing responsibilities and to properly bear meaningful responsibility when allowed. This is what a virtuous man does. This is what a man of high character does. This is what a righteous man does.

The idea that we should pursue a relationship with God is the same idea as devoting ourselves and voluntarily entering into a covenant with God to be righteous and virtuous. When you enter into such a contract, He will forgive you of all shortcomings even when you are not perfectly virtuous because you truly are aiming at a virtuous life. You have repented of all your wrong ways, and are now aiming at pursing the righteousness of God. It is a righteousness that requires us to depend on the Holy Spirit to help us make decisions, and not just the following of simple rules and traditions.

The aim of a virtuous lifestyle should not be fleeting but everlasting. For example, the idea of baptism is not a temporary immersion with results lasting only for a few seconds. Let's look at the Greek word which we translate as baptism in the Bible, "baptizo."[15] The word implies an immersion in order to create a lasting change, as opposed to the word "bapto," which is merely an immersion that has no permanent effect. Greek Poet, Physician and Grammarian Nicander[16] wrote in the 2nd century BC that in order to pickle a vegetable, one must *bapto* (dip without effect) the vegetable in boiling water and then *baptizo* (dip with permanent change) the vegetable in vinegar. A baptizo into the teachings of Jesus would mean permanent transformation. It would mean a permanent commitment.

A covenant needs everlasting devotion. A covenant expects devotion just as you must be devoted for life in marriage. Being good alone does not enter you into such a covenant just as being good to a woman does not make her your wife. In marriage, you must declare your belief, understand what you are entering into and then come to a mutual agreement. There must be a permanent change.

Being virtuous alone has never been good enough for salvation. Jesus needed to die as a sacrifice. And in order to obtain salvation through His sacrifice, we need to follow and devote ourselves to His teachings. I believe that His teachings were to devote ourselves to being virtuous and engage with our conscience and willingly face the meaningful chaos that we can handle.

This is why God told Abraham to leave his country and go explore. This is why Jesus told the Parable of the Talents in which a master gave talents (a form of currency) to three servants and left on a trip. Upon his return, two servants showed that they had invested their talents and returned with more, and the master was pleased with them. But the third servant, who buried his one talent in the ground, was called a wicked and slothful servant. The third servant was afraid of losing money by making the wrong decision, so he played it safe and gave back his one talent. This is not what we are to do! We are not to take what we are given and sit idly. No! We are to take it and try to make the best use of it. It is by engaging in the chaos of life that you can properly handle, with the purpose of creating something beautiful and greater, the conscience and the instincts that God has gifted us.

It is to willingly face chaos and make order out of it. It is to rip the chaos apart and create the heavens and the earth. It is to defeat the enemy and take control of your destiny as best as you can.

And some will say this is wrong because you need to have a personal relationship with God or must know Jesus. I will respond to that by asking you to clarify what you mean by personal relationship or knowing Jesus. Does it mean to know Jesus as you know an acquaintance? Well then, we are too late to meet Him, aren't we? Or does it mean to know His stories? Well, I'm sure you have probably forgotten one parable or one story of Jesus. In fact, I'm sure there were a lot of stories of Jesus that were not recorded (John 21:25). Furthermore, the devil knows the stories of God better than you. The devil believes Jesus exists. The devil has a relationship with God, as he had a long conversation with God in the book of Job. But the devil does not heed the teachings of God. Even those who killed Jesus believed in His existence and knew the basic story of Jesus. So, it cannot simply be a matter of knowing Him or interacting with Him.

Believing in God is to put your faith in the teachings of God. When you have a math teacher that you believe in, you will earnestly try to understand what they teach you and incorporate their teaching into your life as if it is the truth. To say that you accept your teacher is to accept their ways and their teachings.

To believe in Jesus is to believe in the reality of Him as Lord and to accept His main teaching. It is to live virtuously and enter into a covenant with God to always be devoted to such a lifestyle. I see no other logical explanation of what it means to believe in God.

"Assuming that you have heard about him and were taught in him, as the truth is in Jesus, to put off your old self, which belongs to your former manner of life and is corrupt through deceitful desires, and to be renewed in the spirit of your minds, and to put on the new self, created after the likeness of God in true righteousness and holiness."
- Ephesians 4:21–24

So, desire a relationship with God. Make a commitment to be virtuous by bearing meaningful responsibilities and utilizing the instincts that you were born with so that you grow and make better the lives that you love.

CHAPTER 8

"Praiseworthy is whatever seems difficult to a people;
Whatever seems indispensable and difficult is called good;
And whatever liberates even out of the deepest need, the rarest,
the most difficult-that they call holy."
- Friedrich Nietzsche[1]

The Narrow Path

Transcending

We should aim to teach our children to become smart, capable and virtuous so that they can properly live their lives. What does this look like in reality?

We should not say to a young child, who has little understanding of safety and navigation, to go and be free for they will make terrible choices because they need guidance when they are young. Conversely, we should not hope to control every moment of their lives to the extent that they have no freedom or need of their conscience.

We should start with greater control over children by giving them rules. As they grow, we ought to train them to be virtuous and give them responsibilities when they can handle it and are able to use their conscience to make decisions.

For example, parents might tell their children that they need to be in bed by 10 PM every night. This is a good idea as many children do not have the self-control to choose a proper time to go to sleep. But when the children become adults and move out, they need to develop their own understanding of what is right for them in the proper circumstances. If they must stay late at work to finalize a project, then the right thing to do is to stay up past 10 PM and sleep later. Obviously, going to bed on a normal schedule is ideal in most circumstances, and they should try to understand that principle. But as they become adults, they no longer need to follow the strict rules; they can think for themselves and pursue what is actually best. We ought to help children understand the principles of the rules that they are kept under when they are young so that they can actively think about what is ideal and not fall back on the old strict rules that were taught in the beginning.

It is just like virtues (as discussed in the first chapter). Teach them the devotion to a few strict virtues that are generally good. Then when they are old enough to understand the principles, teach them *when* to deviate from the virtues and how to think for themselves. Start with the easy ones, then move on to the more complex ones, like anger, that have nuances that a child would not be able to distinguish. Blindly following some virtues does not make you righteous, just as blindly following some rules does not make you righteous.

A good parent has rules at first but also wants their children to grow up and learn to handle themselves, so when they can move out, they can become a productive individual.

To not teach the process of growing up and taking on the responsibility of thinking for yourself is to be a tyrant who keeps his slaves as an obedient herd of dependent children whom he has power over. It is to go against humanity. It is to prevent someone from transcending the child-like stage and never allowing them to become an adult.

It is in our human nature to become better, more successful, to reproduce, to pass on a legacy and to avoid that which will hinder such goals. Our human nature is to transcend the current state of things and to aim for something better and more admirable. To do anything less is to ignore our instincts and our humanity.

By *instincts,* I do not mean habits or what you were taught from a young age. Instincts are ingrained into our humanity from birth.

We have an instinct to grow, and we cling to that which enables that process. No one taught babies to have natural reactions to hate bitterness and spit out bitter foods. They have an instinct to survive, and they hate that which they assume will make them weaker.

That does not mean that we should always avoid bitter foods, but we should always remember the principle, which is our instinct, of avoiding things that make us weaker. Therefore, feel free to eat bitter foods when you are smart enough to know which bitter foods are safe to consume, but always stay away from that which is actually poisonous. Babies and children ought to be given general guidance in pursuing their instincts, but as they grow up, they are able to more accurately and rationally pursue their instincts.

In the same way, you should separate yourself from those who are evil or those you expect to hurt you more than help. You should always retain the instinct to pursue greatness and the ideal.

When you find yourself in a situation where you must kill or be killed, your instinct is what *motivates* you to load the gun and pull the trigger because you want to live. Your *intellect* is what tells you how to load the bullet and where to squeeze the gun so that the trigger is activated.

It is our human nature, our purpose, to pursue our instincts in the most rational way that we can. We were designed to pursue greatness, and yet, we so often mute our instincts and decide to follow strict rules instead of virtuously and righteously pursuing the ideal.

CULTURAL NORMS

Those who are children ought to live by the norms. Those who are too unwise to understand what the right thing to do is, in other words—those who need a general structure or direction because they are unable to think for themselves about what a man of high character would do, should conform instead of rebelling.

A structure is great for those who are child-like, but it should not be our aim to stay in such a state forever. We should aim to understand the ideas of the norm and then think about each situation. For example, it is generally good to forgive. If you are not capable of understanding if you should forgive or not, then for the sake of creating a cooperative society, the default rule should be to forgive. But if you can understand and are aimed at being virtuous, then you should grow out of such simple ideologies and actually use your conscience to think about what is right and forgive only when you can trust.

We hear things like *"all things in moderation"* and apply it to all circumstances in our lives. We are better off thinking about whether each activity we partake in is actually beneficial or detrimental when we are capable of thinking.

We say that the early bird gets the worm. It may be a good general rule to get up early, but that does not guarantee success. If you get up early and look for worms in the places that everyone dug up yesterday, then you will find nothing. What the phrase ought to be, but is certainly less catchy, is *"the bird that first discovers the novel place with rich potential catches the worm."* Sometimes, entire industries were built by men working till three in the morning and sleeping till noon. You do not have to follow these rules perfectly, but just think about what is actually best.

Yet, some people find comfort in having simple rules direct their entire lives. They would prefer to be ordered by others' opinions of what is best, rather than think on their own. They are slaves who require a master to provide a task. They are the herd. They cling to anything as long as they will not have to utilize their own mind. They say, *"better safe than sorry"* and dare not pursue a worthwhile cause.

Most Christians say that gambling is a sin. But is it not gambling when you start up a company with a 70% chance of failure? Is it not gambling to buy a home and hope that the real estate market goes up? Is it not gambling to invest in stocks and a 401K? It is gambling. But there are certain times when taking risks are appropriate and certain times when they are not. We should use our mind to determine if a risk is worthwhile—and we should take risks when they are worthwhile.

Christianity

To begin looking at how this concept applies to Christianity, we must look at the first story of the Bible. God is the father and His children are in the Garden of Eden. Adam and Eve don't know of their vulnerabilities. Life is easy, and God gives them manageable tasks. They follow the father's rules, and everything works out. They are child-like.

But then the humans encounter something novel which introduces them to fear. The humans have their eyes opened and obtain knowledge of what is truly good and evil and begin to think for themselves. It is the fundamental story of humankind.

The same story is, on a grander scale, played out between the Old and New Testaments of the Bible.

The Old Testament is a book of rules and codes that the Jews adhered to. The first five books of the Old Testament were called *The Torah*, which in Hebrew means *The Law*. It was the childhood version of religion. The laws were strict and were to be adhered to perfectly. God was the Father of the nation of Israel and was building them into a great nation. We can think of the entire Old Testament as a child-like state for the people of Israel. God did not want them to think for themselves until they were developed enough to handle the responsibility of doing so.

> *"I said, 'Obey me and do everything I command you, and you will be my people, and I will be your God. Then I will fulfill the oath I swore to your ancestors, to give them a land flowing with milk and honey'—the land you possess today."*
> - Jeremiah 11:4–5

What does a good father do when his kids are too young to understand if they should forgive their brother? You tell them to forgive each other and to trust each other. And if one forgives and the other continues to misbehave, then you punish the one who misbehaves. Hence, the reason why laws were so strict for Israel. God set up a society where chaos would not ensue, where the children of God would follow His rules so that they could have time to develop into a large nation that could one day become self-sufficient without God's strict rules.

Let's look at the story of Abraham to understand the father–child relationship God had with the people of Israel.[2] The story of Abraham is a story of Abraham's obedience to God. God tells Abraham to leave his country and explore new lands. Abraham obeys. God later tests Abraham by telling him to sacrifice his only son despite his wife and him being very old. Abraham obeys. Abraham takes his son up to an altar and ties his son to it. Abraham grabs his knife to slay his son whom he loved very much but God sends an angel to stop him. Abraham proved his obedience.

God was pleased with Abraham and tells him that a savior will come from his descendants.

So let's bring this back to the idea of going from a child-like state to learning to be virtuous. Abraham proved he was obedient and followed the rules. When a child is obedient, it shows that the child is trying his best to follow what his authority has deemed *good*. When a good parent knows that his child has a good heart and is capable of handling responsibilities, then the parent will begin to bestow responsibilities upon the child. Since the child has been obedient, the parent can have some trust that the child will not abuse the freedom that they have been granted. You can begin to give them the freedom to think for themselves because they will likely use such freedom for *good*.

So God responded to obedience and decided that He could move the people of Israel from the stage of childhood to the stage of adulthood, and the person who would initiate the transition would come from Abraham's lineage because Abraham was obedient and trustworthy. Now, let us fast forward to the New Testament and introduce the Messiah, Jesus, who is a descendant of Abraham.

In the New Testament, which details the life of Jesus and His teachings, Jesus says that the strict parental rules have been removed and shows us the adult version of religion.

The Jews had been adhering to *The Torah* with strict devotion. They followed the laws as best as they possibly could. In Luke 13, we see the story of Jesus preaching in a synagogue on the Sabbath, which went against the law in *The Torah*. The Ten Commandments (which is in *The Torah*) deem the Sabbath to be a day for rest, so when Jesus healed a woman in the synagogue, the priest of the synagogue became angry and told the people that it was unacceptable to receive healing on the Sabbath.

But Jesus was no longer abiding by the childish guidelines. He would do what a man of high character would do and actually use His conscience to think about the right thing to do. He knew that rest was important and understood the value of the principle, but He was no longer confined to the guidelines that were not always ideal. He was a man of high character.

"But now we are released from the law, having died to that which held us captive, so that we serve in the new way of the Spirit and not in the old way of the written code."

- Romans 7:6

Jesus said that the Jews are no longer confined to taking the Sabbath (Saturday) off and no longer banned from eating certain foods or wearing certain clothing. Now, we have no one giving us orders, and we can create our own plans. The strict moral rules are off, but that does not mean that there is no good and evil.

We are no longer tied to The Ten Commandments and the other laws in the Old Testament. It is good to know the old laws and to understand their principles, which may be generally good, but now we can use our conscience to determine what is actually right.

"[Jesus] said to them, 'Therefore every teacher of the law who has become a disciple in the kingdom of heaven is like the owner of a house who brings out of his storeroom new treasures as well as old.'"

- Matthew 13:52

ONLY CHILDREN FOLLOW RULES CREATED BY OTHERS

It is good to have an understanding of the general rules. Proverbs are generalities about what is often true and good. They are not guarantees, which is why Ecclesiastes, the following book that follows Proverbs, takes a more righteous approach and points out the exceptions where following the basic general rules are not ideal. This is where we see the verses which acknowledge that there is a time for each season and a time for each type of action.

We all should have a period where we have general guidance from someone more knowledgeable, but we should aim to leave that stage

147

when we are capable and can aim for righteousness. We should retain the principles of Proverbs, but we should apply rational thinking to determine what is actually right when we are in the next stage.

"So then, the law was our guardian until Christ came, in order that we might be justified by faith."

\- Galatians 3:24

As I have stated in the chapter on the subject regarding affectionate love—follow wise guidance when you are incapable of properly guiding yourself, but when you can use your conscience to determine what is right and ideal, chase what you see is ideal. That is Christianity. That is proper philosophy.

"One repays a teacher badly if one always remains nothing but a pupil."

\- Friedrich Nietzsche[3]

Just knowing the old laws and the child-like rules is not ideal. What is ideal is to understand the good principles of the Old Testament, and then use your own conscience to create an even better world for yourself and others than what the strict rules would have resulted in. Those who follow such a philosophy are the ones who are following what Jesus taught. And those who follow what Jesus taught are meeting one of the requirements for heaven.

"For I tell you that unless your righteousness surpasses that of the Pharisees and the teachers of the law, you will certainly not enter the kingdom of heaven."

\- Matthew 5:20

THE SERMON ON THE MOUNT

In perhaps the most famous of Jesus's teachings, the Sermon on the Mount, we see Jesus provide a new perspective of righteousness for those who have been adhering to the old strict laws. He would tell them the laws that they knew, and then he would introduce a new teaching that they should consider.

The old laws simply said that it was wrong to murder, but Jesus understood the overarching principle that we should not have unjustified anger in any amount. The old law said that you should not commit adultery, but Jesus understood the overarching principle and said that we should not even lust after what belongs to others. The old strict law said to always pay another back an "eye for eye," but Jesus understood the principle of seeking the ideal and knew that sometimes we should punish and sometimes we should forgive, so He showed them that they could sometimes turn the other cheek.

Jesus did not come to abolish the old ways, for sometimes they still were ideal, but He also told them a new way that should also be considered. In other words, do not be only legalistic but also aim for righteousness.

HOLY SPIRIT

This section is for the Christians who believe that we should not use our conscience but rather the Holy Spirit to guide us (John 16:13). My response in short is—I agree that we should follow the Holy Spirit's guidance, but we must use our conscience to discern what revelation is from the Holy Spirit.

Here is a good question to start with: why did Jesus say that it was to our advantage for him to leave so that the Holy Spirit could come (John 16:7)? If the Holy Spirit is one part of the Trinity, why is it advantageous to have the Holy Spirit revealing the truth when the Holy Spirit, compared to Jesus, is harder to decipher and to know if it is truly the revelation of God?

It appears that this would not be to our advantage if the only goal here was to hear the word of God and follow it. But that is not what Jesus came here to do. He understood the philosophy of how to be a proper father. He wanted His children to use their God-given conscience to make decisions. And to do so, He needed to step away. He wanted them to actually be able to wrestle with good ideas and bad ideas and figure out which one was truly best. That is what a good father does. For a good father does not wish to be a wise tyrant over his children forever, but for them to become thinking adults who are aimed at what is good.

What does the Holy Spirit do? It reveals the knowledge of God. It brings us ideas and thoughts.

Think of it this way—where do your ideas and thoughts come from? How is it that you conjure up some idea in your head? There is no way to explain it. If your thoughts stopped coming to you, then you would have no way to make them come back. It is almost random or out of our control. For example, when you are taking a test and are trying to recall a specific sentence from the textbook, you can try to recall what the sentence was to no avail for ten minutes, and then it can randomly pop into your head on your drive home after the test. Are you really in control of your thoughts?

> *"The Spirit searches all things, even the deep things of God. For who knows a person's thoughts except their own spirit within them? In the same way no one knows the thoughts of God except the Spirit of God. What we have received is not the spirit of the world, but the Spirit who is from God, so that we may understand what God has freely given us."*
> - 1 Corinthians 2:10–12

But to actually follow the Holy Spirit, we must use our conscience and knowledge of God's teachings to determine which idea is truly ideal and from God. You can imagine it as having an angel on one shoulder telling you what to do and another spirit on the other shoulder giving you contradictory advice. It is easy when you can actually see the Holy Spirit or Jesus and know that it is from God. But as we cannot see it, we must use our God-given conscience to determine which idea is from God so that the Holy Spirit's advice can be heeded.

And isn't that good? Isn't that to our advantage? Isn't it ideal to separate from our teacher but to retain the ideas and the knowledge of the teacher and decide for ourselves how to best act? Just as a child should grow up and separate from his father at one point, but he should still retain the knowledge and the wisdom of the father and use the knowledge and apply it to future problems.

So refrain from becoming drunk and decreasing your consciousness, so that you may engage with your conscience and hear the ideas of the Holy Spirit.

> *"Therefore do not be foolish, but understand what the will of the Lord is. And do not get drunk with wine, for that is debauchery, but be filled with the Spirit."*

- Ephesians 5:17–18

It may sound peculiar, but the Holy Spirit is an agent that gives us ideas or thoughts. It is up to us to take all of the ideas, compare them to each other and determine which ideas to pursue. Perhaps if we are being led by something that is good and ideal, then the thoughts that pop into our head are more likely to be wisdom that helps us achieve what is in accordance with what we think is ideal.

To say that you believe in God is to subscribe to God's ways, and the Holy Spirit is able to search God's knowledge and bring you His expectations and inform us of right and wrong.

"If, then, I am not convinced by proof from Holy Scripture, or by cogent reasons, if I am not satisfied by the very text I have cited, and if my judgment is not in this way brought into subjection to God's word, I neither can nor will retract anything; for it cannot be either safe or honest for a Christian to speak against his conscience. Here I stand; I cannot do otherwise; God help me! Amen."

- Martin Luther[4]

"When they have a sense of the divine justice added as a witness which allows them not to conceal their sins, but drags them forward as culprits to the bar of God, that sense is called conscience. For it stands as it were between God and man, not suffering man to suppress what he knows in himself; but following him on even to conviction."

- John Calvin[5]

Therefore, do not say that the idea of using your consciousness is flawed, for you must use it to choose the ideas of the Holy Spirit.

THOUGHTS

Descartes wrote, *"I think, therefore I am."*[6]

He was trying to start with the most basic of facts so that he could establish a strong foundation for his studies. He first wanted to establish that he existed. After all, couldn't this all be a dream?

Descartes knew that his thoughts were created, and therefore he concluded that he must exist in order to initiate those thoughts. Even if he doubted that he was thinking, he would then be doubting and therefore he was still thinking. Even if this was all a simulation, those thoughts must be produced from something. Therefore, Descartes claimed that since he was able to think, he must exist on some level.

As a result of this exercise, Descartes was able to conclude "*I think, therefore I am.*"

But do we truly initiate our thoughts? Are we the one creating the thoughts in our own mind? When God spoke to Job in the 38th chapter of Job, God challenged Job's understanding of the things that God does that men do not understand:

"*Who has put wisdom in the inward parts or given understanding to the mind?*"

- Job 38:36

I would say we do not initiate the thoughts, but instead they come to us from God. We are not completely in control of the thoughts that arise in our mind. But we can choose to engage with them and determine if the presented thoughts are worth pursuing. The truth is that Descartes only proved that there is an entity that initiates thoughts, but he did not prove that he was that entity. That is still up for debate.

To use our thoughts as a means of establishing our own existence seems incorrect, and this idea has been refuted by many people before me. If anything, the presence of thoughts proves the existence of some other being (such as the Holy Spirit) as we do not initiate them. Perhaps our ability to receive thoughts gives us a desire to find a god or whatever entity gives us our thoughts. Whatever gives us thoughts must exist and it doesn't seem that they are initiated by us.

THE TRANSCENDENT DOVE

Furthermore, we must recall the mission of a Christian. When you are baptized, it is a sign that you will immerse yourself in chaos and pursue something good and meaningful according to God. It is not to sit still and do nothing but to engage in the world and make a difference. It is to be one who wrestles with God and the ideas He gives you. We must be willing to engage in the worthwhile chaos, which is represented by water, and also be led by the ideas from the Spirit of God.

"Jesus answered, 'Truly, truly, I say to you, unless one is <u>born of</u> <u>water and the Spirit</u>, he cannot enter the kingdom of God.'"
- John 3:5

"Baptism, which corresponds to this, now saves you, not as a removal of dirt from the body but as <u>an appeal to God for a</u> <u>good conscience</u>, through the resurrection of Jesus Christ…"
- 1 Peter 3:20–21

Furthermore, we see that the Holy Spirit is represented by a *dove*. In Luke 3:22, we see *"the Holy Spirit descended on [Jesus] in bodily form like a dove"* as Jesus prays after His baptism. We also see the use of the dove in the story of Noah as the dove searches for land and returns with an olive branch to signify that the water has receded. In both stories, the protagonist has survived the immersing of water, and now, they can throw off the old rules and are given a new life, true vitality, which transcends the old ways. They have transcended, and we see the transcendence upon them in the form of a dove.

We ought to prepare so that we can properly face chaos. These are the type of men that Jesus is calling us to be. We are called to put in the work and be prepared.

Those who are followers of Jesus are those who are *born of the water and the Spirit*. Salvation is only granted to those aiming for the transcendent. But there are those who will try to give you salvation in false ways. You cannot get to heaven by building a tower so tall that it reaches into heaven like the Tower of Babel. Doing so will only lead to more chaos and confusion. We must follow the teachings of Jesus.

Have we noticed what Mark mentions is being sold in the market… the symbol of the transcendence?

"On reaching Jerusalem, Jesus entered the temple courts and began driving out those who were buying and selling there. He overturned the tables of the money changers and the benches of those selling doves, and would not allow anyone to carry merchandise through the temple courts."
- Mark 11:15–16

You cannot buy your religion. You cannot buy the Holy Spirit. You cannot pay to enter heaven. There is no shortcut. You must aim to be a man of high character. You must willingly and bravely face the chaos and be led by what is holy and dare to embrace the meaningful path.

To bravely face chaos when you are prepared is right, or to be put in religious terms—righteous. When John asked Jesus why He needed to be dipped in water, Jesus said, *"It is proper for us to do this to fulfill all righteousness."* In a literal sense, being dipped in water is not crucial to being Christian. Committing to a lifestyle of willingly facing chaos and aiming for something greater is righteous. It is pursuing a proper lifestyle. That is what makes one Christian.

The only way to please God is to have faith (Hebrews 11:6). And yet, Jesus pleased God simply by being baptized. That is because baptism, as we have previously covered, is the display of what it means to have faith in God. To have faith in God is to trust His teaching. It is to create a permanent commitment to virtuously engage in the transcendent. That is faith in God and that is why God was pleased with Jesus's baptism.

The Holy Spirit is a sign of a true man. To ask for the Holy Spirit is to leave the strict rules behind and consciously pursue the ideas of God. Those who engage with the Holy Spirit are those who have chosen to leave childhood and become a man. Those with the Holy Spirit, those aiming at virtuousness, those men of high character—such men have truly lived and are deserving of greatness.

THE TEMPLE

Those who dare to embrace such an endeavor have the Spirit of God within them. Prior to Jesus's death, the Spirit of God usually resided in the temple. Only the priests were allowed to enter the parts of the temple where God's Spirit resided, and the Spirit would speak only to the priests. Then Jesus, the embodiment of the word of God, came to earth.

"And the Word became flesh and dwelt among us, and we have seen his glory, glory as of the only Son from the Father, full of grace and truth."

- John 1:14

The word of God was no longer confined to the temple. Now, the word of God was walking around earth and sharing the knowledge of God.

"So the Jews said to him, 'What sign do you show us for doing these things?' Jesus answered them, 'Destroy this temple, and in three days I will raise it up. The Jews then said, 'It has taken forty-six years to build this temple, and will you raise it up in three days?' But he was speaking about the temple of his body."

- John 2:18–21

Then Jesus was crucified. The temple curtains were torn down by God. The revelation of God was no longer only accessible to the priests who passed through the curtains or those who spoke directly to Jesus but forevermore to all who desired to hear the word of God. In fact, we now have the potential to hear the word of God within ourselves. We have been taught and shown the proper path to live through Jesus; therefore, we can now use our own conscience to be led by God to guide us to do what is right as we engage in the chaos of this world. We now have something within ourselves that allows God to speak to us directly.

"Do you not know that you are God's temple and that God's Spirit dwells in you?"

- 1 Corinthians 3:16

SANCTIFICATION

I have stated that being a Christian means devoting yourself and entering into God's covenant to aim to be virtuous. Let me back this claim up here with some verses.

"But thanks be to God, that <u>you who were once slaves of sin have become obedient</u> from the heart to the standard of teaching to which you were committed, and, having been set free from sin, <u>have become slaves of righteousness</u>. I am speaking in human terms, because of your natural limitations. For just as you once presented your members as slaves to impurity and to lawlessness leading to more lawlessness, <u>so now present your members as slaves to righteousness leading to sanctification</u>."

- Romans 6:17–19

These verses tell us that those who are Christians are those who have committed to a standard of teaching which is righteous. This commitment to righteousness will lead to sanctification (which is becoming *more holy*).

So then we ought to look at what it means to be a *"slave to righteousness."* Righteousness, defined as *"doing what is morally right,"* is essentially the same thing as virtuousness. Virtuousness is doing what a man of high character would do, and isn't Jesus a man of high character? Why do we say that Jesus's anger was righteous when He exhibited it, but we still do not consider anger to be a virtue? Both terms refer to engaging with the Spirit of truth to search for what is righteous. Righteousness is virtuousness.

> *"Brothers and sisters, my heart's desire and prayer to God for the Israelites is that they may be saved. For I can testify about them that they are zealous for God, but <u>their zeal is not based on knowledge</u>. Since they did not know the righteousness of God and sought to establish their own, they <u>did not submit to God's righteousness.</u> Christ is the culmination of the law so that there may be righteousness for everyone who believes."*
>
> - Romans 10:1–4

This tells us that being excited and enthusiastic and affectionate about God will not save you. You must know God's teachings and what it means to be righteous. You must know what it means to be properly virtuous so that you can be imitators of God, who is perfectly righteous.

Or shall we rely on strict rules like the Pharisees? No! For Jesus came to free us from the strict law and give us the Holy Spirit and conscience to determine what is right. Righteousness is to do what God would do, what Jesus would do, what a man of high character would do.

> *"All Scripture is breathed out by God and profitable for teaching, for reproof, for correction, and for training in righteousness, that the man of God may be complete, equipped for every good work."*
>
> - 2 Timothy 3:16–17

> *"By this it is evident who are the children of God, and who are*

*the children of the devil: whoever does not practice righteousness
is not of God, nor is the one who does not agapē his brother.*"
- 1 John 3:10

Despite claiming to be Christian, do we actually aim for righteousness? Or do we aim for the easy, the unconditional, the simple, the unthoughtful, the linear, the wide path that covers a sufficient ground for us to manage to usually get through life?

We were not called to aim for that. We were called to aim for righteousness, perfection, to engage with each virtue properly—not blindly and without thought.

FRIEDRICH NIETZSCHE (1844–1900)

Friedrich Nietzsche, who was a fierce critic of Christianity, was one of the most influential thinkers to impact Western philosophy. Nietzsche was the famous German philosopher who coined the terms *"God is dead"* and *"He who has a why to live can bear almost any how."* He thought Christians were child-like who only preached strict obedience to certain rules that were not always ideal. Christians were one of the groups that were kept tame and child-like, or as he labeled them, *the herd.*[7]

Nietzsche believed that Christians were creating excuses and doctrines to justify their standing and not actually striving to be virtuous. They were too poor to have great things, so they created a rule that said that we should not envy, making Christians feel superior, even though they had less. They say to always forgive because they are too weak or cowardly to actually hold others accountable.

In some ways, Nietzsche was right. Christians, too often, are no longer virtuous. They cling to strict rules and often do not preach virtues properly. Too often, pastors say that we should never fear, be selfish or have pride, but instead to give and sacrifice for your neighbor. And this is dogmatically taught throughout the church. They are not told to think about when to be anxious, when to forgive or when to be selfish. They are told to follow strict rules.

He believed, and rightly so, that Christians were trying to divest themselves of their instincts.[8] Instead of actually contemplating what was right or wrong, they just closed their eyes and mind and relied on their *faith* for an answer.

No wonder he was such a critic of Christianity. Christians are too often taught to be child-like throughout their adulthood. They are deprived of humanity. They are the herd.

But I must stress that this is not what I believe Christianity teaches. I do believe it teaches us to leave the child-like state and become virtuous. But I must admit that Nietzsche was right that Christians are not taught this throughout the church.

Übermensch (Overman)

In Nietzsche's book *The Gay Science* (titled after a common phrase at the time meaning 'The Joyful Wisdom'), Nietzsche tells the story of a man coming into a town where he seeks God. But the citizens of the town mock him and tell him that God is not there for they no longer believe in God. After much commotion, the man tells the citizens that they have killed God.

When Nietzsche said that *"God is dead,"*[9] he meant that society no longer had an ideal, a belief system or a correct moral standard that they ought to follow. He realized that people had replaced God's doctrine with their own philosophy. Yet, Nietzsche knew that this is nothing to celebrate, for this would lead to despair and chaos for the masses. Without a solid structure or standard to guide them, what are they to do? Which direction are they to go? How are they to act?

In *The Gay Science*, Nietzsche reflects on *"The greatest recent event-that 'God is dead'; that the belief in the Christian God has become unbelievable."* He explains that *"many people might know what has really happened here, and what must collapse now that this belief has been undermined-all that was built upon it, leaned on it, grew into it; for example, our whole European morality..."*[10]

He predicted that what was to come was the *"succession of demolition, destruction, downfall... this monstrous logic of horror,... which has probably never before existed on earth."*[11]

With the advent of the enlightenment era, people were creating their own theories on morality, beyond the simple *good and evil* that the Christian preachers taught. Some people would thrive under their new philosophies, people Nietzsche called the *Übermensch*, and others would be devastated without guidance and fall into nihilism leading to a lack of morality and structure in society.

Nietzsche wrote another book called *Thus Spoke Zarathustra*. The book told the story of a wise man who came into a town where he tells the citizens the ways of the *Übermensch*. He teaches them a new morality—the proper way to be virtuous. But to learn a new way of living would mean to go against current morality and what people *categorically* have established as good and evil.

Sometimes, the *Übermensch* was proud of himself; sometimes, he used violence at times, and he even thought that anger was ideal sometimes. Even though anger is considered immoral, evil and categorically bad by the masses, a truly virtuous man would show it at the proper time because he knows it can be useful for good. Even things that the majority would consider to be a sin, a man of high character would do if it was virtuous. He would not be constrained to the group thought, but instead he would be an individual who thinks for himself because he is capable of bearing such responsibility.

Nietzsche did not ask how the old ways would be preserved, no. He asked how they would be overcome. He wanted to know how to be better and leave the old ways that said violence, fear and anger were always bad and find a more virtuous philosophy.

Nietzsche thought that those who were the *Übermensch* would be a different breed of humans. They would not be confined to thoughtless norms that society followed. No, they were the adults. The individuals who actually thought and lived freely and virtuously.

The idea that we need to transcend, that is to move from childhood to adulthood and to leave strict rules so that we can become virtuous, is proper philosophy. I also believe that it is a key principle of Christianity. However, Nietzsche did not see Christianity as a virtuous belief structure. He deemed the beliefs that were taught dogmatically to be non-ideal, nihilistic and encouraging conformity as opposed to individuality.

NIETZSCHE ON CHRISTIANS

Nietzsche claimed that the church wants the typical religious man to seek the mediocre.[12] He is right. Most do not like a complicated structure for which we must think and use our full cognitive abilities. Most only want what is black and white—sacrificing true excellence for simplicity. When things are curved, we take the derivative to allow everyone to comprehend the idea—sacrificing the grandeur and the height of reality.

And that is what the church was teaching and continues teaches to this day. We simplify everything and blind ourselves to the verses that tell us to think. We choose to take non-ideal philosophies that are easy enough for a child to understand. Yes, I will always forgive. No, I will never fear. No, I will never judge. How is this to our advantage?

Nietzsche says in *The Antichrist*, "*I call an animal, a species, or an individual corrupt when it loses it instincts, when it chooses, when it prefers, what is disadvantageous for it.*"[13] No wonder he likened Christianity to nihilism. We were choosing to not be great. We do not promote becoming a great man and being virtuous.

Nietzsche's main criticism of Christianity is that the God of the New Testament lacked "*wrath, revenge, envy, scorn, cunning, violence*" [14] and was, therefore, undeserving of respect. He viewed the God of the Old Testament with strength and power. But as Christians have begun to value meekness, pity and being incapable, they have also turned their God into a weak God incapable of such virtues.[15] He said that the New Testament God has become "*timid and modest; he counsels 'peace of soul,' hate-no-more, forbearance, even 'love' of friend and enemy.*"[16]

This is what many Christians now preach. But I do not believe Jesus taught this nor do I believe we have a powerless God. I believe we still have a God who is wrathful and who has never taught us to *always forgive in our hearts* so that we can have "*peace in our soul.*" The Christian God is one who hates the wicked. Yet, it is a rare Christian who will dare say that he is allowed to hate a person.

Hate is a strong word. The weaker man will cling to this cliché and never say or feel it. The greater man wields all that he is capable of that gives him the greatest strength and will only use it in the proper circumstance. He wants every powerful tool in his capability. This is why God is capable of these terrifying virtues.

Our God did not teach us to have the same love for our friends and enemies. Yes, we should have an *agapē* for both, but that does not mean I will sacrifice for my enemy. Yet, the church still tells us to love our enemy and gives us no context as to the type of love. We have chosen the childish ideology of clinging to the *unconditional* at our own fault because we are too weak to dare to think for ourselves and aim for righteousness.

We have applied these sheepish attributes to our God even though He has not changed. We have killed our God with our unbelief in who He truly is. We have forgotten Him and turned to a new golden calf that reflects what we want only moments after He showed us how great his ways are.

Can you blame Nietzsche for disliking Christians? Nietzsche knew what was useful and what led to decay. He saw that many Christians were, and still are, teaching that which leads to decay.

No wonder he said that *"God is dead"* and not *"God never existed."*

Can you truly blame Nietzsche for disliking the false God of the New Testament that has been dogmatically taught? The Bible says to have *agapē* for your God, but shouldn't your god be perfect to meet your standards for a god? Therefore, why should Nietzsche respect and associate with a god that does not meet the standards of a righteous god? The god that we have been preaching is not perfect. He is weak and pathetic and not worthy of being God.

We act as if our God has changed from the days of the Old Testament, but He hasn't. Only the rules that pertain to us have changed as we have been granted freedom as we have grown past the childhood stage. We act as if He was the God who was capable of wrath but now is only a God of love and kindness and toleration— but this is not true. He is still a God of wrath and envy and judgment. We only focus on the fact that He is *agapē*, and we interpret *agapē* in such a way that we expect Him to lavish us with mercy and grace when we do not deserve them.

WEAKNESS

The religious used to idealize that which was powerful and capable but now aim at that which is weak. It is no surprise that

Christians often see pity as an absolutely good virtue. We have aimed at weakness and the non-ideal. The weaker we are, the more we think we are virtuous and more holy. Many think we ought to be poor to have a chance to get into heaven. We say that those who are *meek will inherit the earth* as if the verse meant that only the weak and timid will succeed. Do you see why Nietzsche called Christianity the religion of pity and nihilism?[17] We appear to be the religion promoting incapability and weakness.

This interpretation is bad teaching. The Greek word, *praus*, that has been translated into "*meek*" is not the word to describe something weak and timid. It is the word used to describe a war-horse. It is the word to describe something with great power and capabilities, yet in control and used properly. And yet, we still say that God blesses those who are meek.

So do not be like the others that call themselves Christians and merely follow along blindly as sheep. That was never the intention of Christianity. Stop saying *amen* and *hallelujah* until you actually know what you are saying! Or would you rather just keep your eyes closed and sing meaningless words because you have been told to? I sincerely hope you choose wisely and use the God-given gifts that you were bestowed and live to your full potential. I hope that you actually question the things you are told and seek the truth. I hope you build yourself up and do not tear yourself down.

I hope that you believe in a God that is righteous and powerful, not one that is weak and timid. So let us no longer preach of a God that is weak and childish. No! Let us preach of a God who is great and virtuous and right in all things.

PURSUIT OF INSTINCTS

Let us take a step back and return to the idea of beginning as a child and following rules, but then as we become capable of handling responsibilities we are allowed to transcend into the adult stage of life.

Again—follow wise guidance when you are incapable of properly guiding yourself, but when you can use your conscience to determine what is right and what is ideal, chase what you see is ideal. That is Christianity. That is Nietzsche's *Übermensch*. Both are promoting the greater man—a man of high character.

We should obey the authority (like parents, teachers, cultural norms, natural reactions, etc.) in the beginning and then deviate from their strict rules and general guidance as we become capable of pursuing a more righteous way.

While all of the authorities can potentially update their perspectives of the ideal, our natural reactions is the only authority within ourselves that we can change. We can acquire new tastes; we can love what we were once scared of; we can subdue our fears that are not dangerous. Our natural reactions, with enough practice, can morph into our most recent actions of rationality.

There are two stages of life—following along and thinking for yourself. It is not ideal to always think for yourself, but you should always aim to get to the place where you should think for yourself. The two stages are proper for a certain time as they can both serve as the optimal means of pursuing greatness, survival, power and leaving a legacy—your instincts.

Why pursue instincts? Because we were created to do so. The natural release of serotonin and euphoria by achieving our instinctual desires is nature's or God's—whatever you believe was the reason for your creation—way of telling you to pursue your instincts. We were designed to feel joy in the pursuit of our instincts so that we may continually pursue them.

All men are born with the same instincts. Why? I do not yet know.

I know that when I touch a burning hot stove, I naturally react before I am rationally able to understand what I am doing—and that is good. In the cases when I am unable to understand what is ideal, I allow my wise guide (in this case—natural reaction) to guide me. I am like a child, unable to comprehend the ideal in a reasonable time, so under such circumstances, I follow the rules of the wise guide. In the same way, *I will act on my natural instincts to live a great and meaningful life while I am here, even though I have yet to rationally figure out exactly why I am here.*

When the greater man clearly sees and knows the ideal he pursues it. When the greater man is unable to identify the ideal, he heeds the advice of the wise guardian who offers guidance. When it comes to the question of why we were put on this earth, perhaps we will never know. Until we know, follow the wise guide of our instincts.

Therefore, choose to live, reproduce, and become greater as long as you are capable of doing so.

MORALITY

Most Christians, atheists and agnostics do believe that some things are immoral and wrong. We all see the death of a good person as a tragedy that we wish would not have happened. We see someone succeed and we are generally happy and we tell them they are on the right path. Every human was born with a deep understanding that there is an ideal, and unnecessary cruelty and the destruction of great things are not consistent with such an ideal. This is because we were all born with instincts and we determine something to be moral when it is contributing to our instincts and immoral when it goes against the rational pursuit of instincts.

We must know how morality is determined. Why is it that gambling in a casino is immoral, yet starting a business with a 70% chance of failure (which is a gamble) is not inherently immoral? In short, because the business can be a rational attempt at bettering your life, while the other one is an irrational attempt that is often not worthwhile.

Why is it that we all know that an anorexic person or a glutton are not considered to be living in the ideal manner? Why is it that the majority thinks the right thing to do is be healthy and we look down on those who do not aim for good health? Because morality is based on the rational pursuit of instincts—to survive, to become great, to reproduce. To disregard your health is to not be aiming at your instincts.

The question remains: where do our instincts come from? I believe they come from God and that these instincts are to be respected and adhered to and pursued as optimally as possible. If you believe you were intelligently designed, then ask yourself: how was I designed? What was I instilled with from birth?—instincts. Therefore, I do believe that God has given us morality and the knowledge of good and evil.

Morality is subject to what is rationally best for our instincts. Killing another human is sometimes moral and sometimes immoral. Even lying can be considered righteous (James 2:25) when it is done to preserve the lives of those you care about, as we see in the biblical story of Rahab.[19] Perhaps morality could be said to be relative in the sense that what is best for our instincts is relative to the circumstances.

It is important to understand what is moral and immoral, so that we can properly live our lives with some structure that allows us to know the ideal. God is not going to tell us whether each individual case is moral or immoral; therefore, we must have a way of knowing how to determine what is moral and immoral—hence, we were born with instincts.

In short—we must have an ideal if we are to make any meaningful decisions. Believers believe in God and base what is meaningful based on *His will* (which I would consider to be the rational pursuit of instincts). Trust the understanding that God has given us from birth to seek righteousness.

"Trust in the Lord with all your heart, and do not lean on your
own understanding.
In all your ways acknowledge him, and he will make straight
your paths."
- Proverbs 3:5-6

Can our instincts conflict? Absolutely. Sometimes a parent will sacrifice themselves for their child. This is because the parent considers himself to be one with the child. He cares more about the net benefit between the two and he will lay his life down to keep his child alive. The main instinct we have is to live to the fullest. To squeeze out the maximum from our time on earth. To achieve the greatest that we can bear, this is what pleases God and brings us honor. And by keeping your children alive and preparing them to live properly, they are a part of you that will continue to live on and achieve great things.

"to those who by patience in well-doing seek for glory and honor
and immortality, he will give eternal life."
- Romans 2:7

We all were born with this instinct. It is the law of God that was written on our hearts from birth. Even those who are not religious have this natural law from birth, even though they have not explicitly heard the law from God.

"For it is not the hearers of the law who are righteous before
God, but the doers of the law who will be justified.
For when Gentiles, who do not have the law, by nature do what
the law requires, they are a law to themselves, even though they
do not have the law.
"They show that the work of the law is written on their hearts,
while their conscience also bears witness, and their conflicting
thoughts accuse or even excuse them"
- Romans 2:13-15

DESIGNED FOR GREATNESS

Most Christians are running from their instincts. Most are told to follow a new set of strict rules which do not contribute to their instincts and are rarely told to think for themselves.

They begin to feel bitter against someone, which they consider categorically evil, and ignore the bitterness. Bitterness is a natural reaction we have towards things that are poisonous and allows us to be aware of things that may harm us. We should listen to our instincts to stay away from that which harms us. Yet, we are told to completely ignore such things and always forgive! We are told to never get angry or jealous. No! What foolish nihilists are we! We ought to learn that as long as something is poisonous, we will not engage with it until it changes and is no longer poisonous. Instead we ignore our instincts and swallow poison and say it's the right thing to do because this is what many pastors preach.

That is the exact opposite of what Jesus taught! He taught us to listen to our natural guide and also use our conscience when we are capable. Instead, we mute the guides and disengage from our conscience.

I hope you have enough instinct left in you to be repulsed by those who tell you to *be yourself*, for they preach nihilism. I hope you have enough instinct in you to know that you should always aim to be greater than you currently are. I hope you have the courage to look to the great models who have come before and do as they would have done if they were in your shoes.

We were designed to be great. Some will say that the human condition is one that wants comfort and the status quo—this is wrong. We instinctually prefer the status quo only when we see no better option. The human condition also beckons us to aim for greatness when it is available. We feel a rush of serotonin when we try something novel because our design is beckoning us to explore new paths that may lead to greatness. We were designed to be great men! The natural state of man is pursuing the ideal. Sometimes, that means change and growth and sometimes, standing still. The natural state of man is to be virtuous. But we have become corrupted.

We have muted our instincts. We have decided to live a life where we are always rebelling or always conforming. We have rationalized our way out of greatness. We were not made for such meekness. No! The human condition, the man made in God's image, the man of high character is one who pursues greatness and persists along the best path.

Follow the status quo when you see no better option but also listen to the ideas that pop in your head that beckon you to greatness and decide if they are worthwhile and persist with the ideas that bring you to greatness. We should only use "*always*" in the pursuit of our principles in the most ideal manner available.

"*Steadfastness should be for the will, not the mind.*"
- Baltasar Gracián[19]

You must have the old principles and the intellect of the present. You must have the instincts of humanity and the rationality of heaven.

A SOLID FOUNDATION (INSTINCTUAL I)

We must be instinctual. We must retain the purpose that we were born with. We were not a blank slate, but designed with instincts that are burning in the background of our lives. Some blow out their flame. They cannot justify their existence or why they should even bother living. For this reason, it is important to have a solid grounding, a solid foundation, to be in touch with your instincts.

Reconnect with your instincts. Go be in nature. Go watch a meaningful movie that motivates you and speaks to you. Talk with family and friends. Take a walk in nature. Study someone who is pursuing the righteousness of God. Participate in the rituals and traditions that have proven to bring you stability in times of chaos. Read a book that tells the heroic story of man overcoming great obstacles and creating a better world. Read the book of your religion. Hold your newborn baby and discover your purpose in life. These are the things that remind us of our instinctual purpose in life and give us a general push in the right direction. These moments that reconnect us with our foundation do not save us, just as traditions and rituals do not save us. But they remind us and reorient us towards our purpose of life.

Sometimes, we need to see a story of a man go from rags to riches. And that motivates us to get a job and start providing for our family. We must remind ourselves of our instinctual desires and the joy that pursuing them brings.

However, we should not see the pursuit of instincts being done in one manner, and think that we should replicate it for eternity—we must be rational. We must get out of the strict rule of "always chase money" and consciously consider if we have enough money; if we do have enough money, we should spend more time pursuing other goals that will better contribute to our instincts. Are you an individual who thinks rationally? Or are you one who stays in the herd and blindly follows along and does not question the initial nudge that life has given you to go in a certain direction?

It is good to be moved by your passions at first; they should steer you towards greatness and love. But are you to be Romeo and only live solely in your passions? Should you let your life fall apart when you cannot have your passions? No! Let them motivate you, but then be rational! Think!

We should not only look at potential partners and rely on passions to determine if they would be a worthwhile partner but also investigate and talk with them and see if they are intelligent, compassionate, conscientious, industrious, consistent and trustworthy.

Do not completely trust your passions. We are passionate for that which we assume will contribute to our instincts. Do apply all of the rational thought you have at your disposal to make sure that your passions will actually contribute to your instincts.

Likewise, it is generally good to be aware of your fears and to respond to them (natural reaction), but the man of high character responds to his fears (natural reaction) and also consciously engages with his rationality to do what is best (transcends).

Likewise, when you have romantic passions for someone and also rationally realize that that the two of you are compatible and are willing to be embark on the path of marriage, then you have love on a different level. You have something transcendent and beautiful. You have *true love*.

Love at first sight is one example of the instinctual attraction that is necessary for *true love*. I do not believe that *love at first sight* is sufficient for creating *true love*, but I do believe that *love at first sight* (or some level of instinctual attraction) is required for *true love*.

It is not only the passion and the lust and the instinct to reproduce but also the rational mind that analyzes your compatibility with each other. It is not only the rational choice of trust and compatibility but also the instinctual passion you must have for your partner.

We ought to stop uttering meaningless phrases such as "*follow your heart.*" How much less confused might we be if instead we were told to "*rationally pursue your instincts!*"

Nihilism (Instinctual II)

To ignore our instincts and be purely rational will only lead to nihilism. When we look at the world from a purely rational stance, we will see no difference in what we do now because in 10,000 years, humanity will be no more. Why have children? Why aim for something great if it will one day turn to dust? Why suffer and invest in life if it will have no value one day? Why should we love one another? The only answer to these questions is because we have the instincts to do such things.

To depend only on logic and rationality will not provide the motivation to use your logic or rationality. You must have some reason for being on earth. As we were not made with a blank slate, but instead pre-programmed with human instincts, I believe that pursuing our innate instincts as righteously as possible is what we were designed to do here on earth; I believe that is God's will for our lives. I cannot tell you why, only that we were created to do so.

When we do not pursue our instincts and what is advantageous to our growth and advancement, then, according to Nietzsche, we have been *corrupted*. According to the Bible, we have *iniquity*. To have iniquity is to become twisted in our thinking. It is to become muted to our instincts. It is to be corrupt in our nature. It is to have walked away from being made in the image of God.

A wise suitor—the man of high character—will only pursue someone who also yearns to fulfill their instincts, as such a person will choose to love, reproduce and also aim for greatness. To willingly and knowingly marry someone who hinders your instinctual pursuit is to limit your aim.

There are some who say that they did not willingly make such a choice or that they no longer believe they can live a life of pursuing certain human instincts. They claim that they are doing the best they can with what they currently have, therefore, it is not a sin—and perhaps it is not a sin from your perspective. However, even if you do not see it as a sin, you must see it as an iniquity.

To sin is to miss the mark, to be faulty in *rationality* and execution. Iniquity is to be crooked in your aim, to lack even a proper aim, to refrain from pursuing your *instincts*.

Perhaps it is that we only focus on our sins as being the only thing that bar us from entering heaven. Yet, it is sins, transgressions (breaking trust) and iniquities that can each separate us from the perfection that God demands. We must not forget that our iniquities, our crooked ways, our failings to pursue our God-given human instincts are also shortcomings that have deadly consequences.

To refrain from pursing the ideal in order to not fail is still a failure.

Heaven is not only for those who lack a record of sins or transgressions. Heaven requires a proper aim. Heaven is for those who have been baptized with the commitment to dare to pursue the ideal.

It is not enough in life to say that you have done nothing and therefore are deserving of greatness. No! We must first have a proper aim. We must engage with the instincts we humans have been granted and pursue them with vigor. Then, when our aim is proper, we can focus on how to best achieve our aim. We must have a proper aim (instincts) and do our best to achieve it (rationality).

We know those who are not rationally pursuing their instincts have become corrupted. If a person chooses to never eat or to overeat, we know that they have a serious problem and are not going about the instinct of survival in a rational way. Something has confused their natural instinct to survive and to better themselves and they have obtained a new understanding of an ideal. They have a new aim: an aim to be skinny, an aim to feel the joy of food. We know this is immoral because they are ignoring the pursuit of their instincts, which they ought to aim for with rationality. We should never encourage someone to disregard instincts.

The same idea should be applied to sexuality. If someone chooses a lifestyle of sleeping with someone that they cannot reproduce with, we know that they are not going about their instinct of reproducing in a rational way. The truth is that something has corrupted them. Just as an anorexic girl may think her new lifestyle is ideal and she ought to not eat, one who does not choose a partner of the opposite sex finds their situation ideal.

How can you tell someone that their aim is not the ideal? I do not think you can do so without providing a clear definition of a better aim. Only then can you compare the two. To only tell someone that their way is wrong, will only irritate them unless you actually provide proof that a different way is better. Perhaps a corrupted person can see that in the areas that they do rationally pursue their instincts they feel the most long-lasting joy.

How do people deal with their own iniquities? Either by being ashamed or proud. Many who are physically corrupted feel a sense of loss. They may have lost the ability to reproduce or think properly and achieve great things again. Those who have been corrupted by circumstance should do their best to continually pursue what instincts they have left. Those who have been corrupted by choice and are still capable of their instincts ought to pursue them rationally.

And then there are those that embrace their iniquities and become proud. They invite others to join them in their lack of pursuing their instincts, as if it was the ideal. What have they to be proud of? No athlete would be proud and celebrate a career-ending injury. Only one who hated the game would do such a thing. Those who are proud of their corruption are nihilists deep down or live according to a morality that is contrary to the rest of the world. They do not pursue their instincts, which all morality is based on.

Perhaps, even having an iniquity alone is a sin. Those who are aiming at the wrong thing may have hit their mark, but they are missing the target that God is looking at, and in God's perspective it would be a sin.

We say that a sin is missing the mark, and this is true. But most importantly, we must know what we are aiming at. We must first know that we ought to aim at rationally pursuing our instincts.

Regress (Instinctual III)

On the other hand, to go too far to the other extreme by rejecting rationality and solely pursue instincts is also a childish ideology. To be purely instinctual is to *regress*. It is to ignore the most rational and ideal way of going about instincts. It is to act in the short-term desire that may harm our long-term desires. This would be a regression from the human state back to the animalistic state. You must strive for both instinct and rationality! You must have instinctual desires and must aim to be as rational as possible in the pursuit of those desires. To have only rationality is to be corrupted and to have only instinct is to be regressed.

We are incorrect when we say that personality is all that matters. That is corrupt thinking. We must not forget our instinct to choose to love one who is able to reproduce and who we find to be the best partner (that we can attain) for such a task based on physical attributes. And on the other hand, to say that physical beauty is all that matters is childish, regressive thinking as you have not bothered to rationally consider the personality and the compatibility of such a partner. You must care about physical beauty and personality. You must be instinctual and as rational as possible.

Why We love (Instinctual IV)

We were designed to love that which we expect to contribute to our instincts.

The man of high character loves because he was born with the natural reaction to love. He was born with the natural reaction to cling to that which he believes will contribute to his other instincts. Love is the guide that allows us to pursue all other instincts optimally, given we love rationally.

You should always cling to that which benefits your instincts, no matter the past. If you trust that it is now useful, then disregard the past. This is ideal to pursuing your instincts. This is why we have *agapē*. We should always have a desire to cling to that which we trust is for our betterment.

This magical feeling, this unexplainable phenomenon, this joy we experience that we know as the feeling of love—it is our reward for pursuing our instincts. We feel joy when we accomplish a great task, for that is the result of pursuing our instinct to be great. We feel joy when a baby is born, for that is the result of pursuing our instinct to continue a part of us. We feel joy when we find someone who wants the best for us and is willing to stay by our side, for that is the result of pursuing our instinct to cling to that which is better for us—love.

Pursuing our instincts brings joy. The rational pursuit of instincts brings an everlasting love.

In order to love maximally, rationally pursue your instincts. If you feel you do not love, rationally pursue your instincts, and you will find that you love that which contributes to the pursuit of your instincts.

This is equally applicable to spouses if they wish to become the deep desire of their spouse. Be supportive of the other in their pursuit of their instincts if you wish to obtain their love.

To discourage or tear someone away from the pursuit of their instincts should only be done under extreme circumstances when the pursuit of certain instincts will lead to significant harm. This goes for all types of relationships, from individual relationships to the relationships politicians have with their constituents.

Perhaps it is that we also tear ourselves from our instincts. We confuse our body by making it think it is pursuing its instincts, but only artificially. We have sex without a partner or a meaningful partner, take drugs to feel the rush of life and scrounge for attention without actually achieving anything worthwhile. This joy only lasts so long before we subconsciously realize its artificiality and that such things do not contribute to our instincts.

Aim to be rational in order to be sure that you are contributing to your instincts and not some synthetic version that temporarily tricks your body into thinking it is on the path to fulfilling its instincts. Being rational allows you to continue loving and pursuing your instincts for the longest time.

We must pursue our true instincts of being great—not living great but being great. Doing. Creating. This is why coddling is not love. It does not allow the other person to pursue their instincts properly, but instead provides an artificial happiness that does not actually come as a result of the individual properly pursuing their instincts.

Perhaps, sometimes, coddling someone can remind them of joy, but it should only be done with the purpose of reigniting their passion for life, not to make them happy.

Is it wrong to do things that are artificial? Is it wrong to do things that do not contribute to our instincts? Sometimes. If the artificial activity removes or seriously risks confusing your desire or ability to pursue your instincts, then it is immoral. If it brings happiness while not hindering or taking the place of the rational pursuit of your instincts, then it is acceptable.

If You Love Her, Be Willing to Let Her Go (Rational I)

The man of high character is instinctual and rational. To lack one of these is to lack the greatest version of an affectionate love.

Those who lack rationality are not ideal people to pursue. A rational man knows that if he is dating someone, then there are potential reasons to let a woman go. For example, she may not love him. Yet, many are unwilling to let someone go. They are only acting on their passions and lack the rationality to realize that there might be a legitimate reason to let go of someone they used to date. They are full of pure passion and instinct.

If you don't have the rational capability to let someone go at the proper time, then you aren't acting with enough rationality. You have insufficient rationality in your love for her.

And you need both passion and rationality to fully love someone! If you lack rationality, then you are not loving someone properly. You are a child who only pursues their passions, which may not actually be ideal for you or her. *You are not concerned about the other person and actually want the best for them but only want to satisfy your own passions.* If you truly love her, then you will let her go if she truly wants to go.

And no woman wants to have a romantic relationship with a child. Your pursuit of her will only push her further away. A good woman wants a man who is passionately in love, yet rational and wise and desires what is best for her.

A weak woman wants a man who will chase after her when he shouldn't. She will want a man who is so instinctually and passionately in love that he is blind to rationality. But such a woman is not the women you ought to desire. You should desire a woman who is mature enough to desire a man who is passionate and rational. A woman of high character should desire a rational and passionate man.

Only a rational man is capable of a long-term relationship. During marriage, many passions will arise, but you must be rational and think about what is actually right. You should not leave your wife for another who is also attractive. No. You must also rationally think about your vows and your children.

To be purely instinctual is to sleep with whichever woman will take you for the night. Yet, we need the instinctual passion to motivate us to find a spouse. Rationality allows you to see the value and benefits of long-term friendships.

Lastly, it is not those who are content with their lives that are ready for true love. True love is for those who have desires and strive to fulfill the void of a partner that their instincts beckon for. True love is for those who have a burning instinct that motivates their pursuit and have developed the ability to think rationally under the pressure of motivation to choose the right partner. Yet, the weaker man will say to only utilize only one because he lacks the ability to properly handle both at the same time. But in choosing to utilize only the rationality, he risks never finding love because he is unmotivated to search for it. In choosing only to utilize instinct, he risks ending up with someone he is not compatible with. The man of high character develops himself enough so that he can bear both instinct and rationality at the same time—pursuing true love properly.

SUPERIOR (RATIONAL II)

We are not purely savage beasts or men who are only wired to respond to primitive stimuli! No! We have the passion and capability of beasts while harnessing the ideas of God within us if we choose to utilize them.

You must be someone who is not only motivated by your innate passions but also acts as rationally as possible in your pursuit.

> *"...the things which have life are superior to those which have not life, and of those which have life the superior are those which have reason."*
>
> - Marcus Aurelius[20]

We should not pursue our instincts like cavemen by killing and plundering others' land to better our lives, for this lacks rationality. We have laws that will put you in jail if you steal from your neighbor. And even if there were no laws, we are most often better off when we work with others and focus on fostering synergistic pursuits and respecting those that also aim to produce and live virtuously. This is why we should not take over other countries or steal from our neighbor, unless they are working against us and pose a significant threat.

Perhaps we will be forgiven for our lack of rationality if we are incapable of it. I believe a child should be forgiven if he has good intentions but is unable to rationally choose the ideal method. I believe Jesus showed us that the soldiers who killed him would be forgiven for they had the proper motivation (doing their job), but were unaware of exactly what they were doing because they were not involved in the judicial process. But if you are capable of being rational and knowing what the ideal is, then you bear a great responsibility and will be held accountable for that which you have been given.

TRUE BELIEF (RATIONAL III)

There may be times when we are unwillingly separated or out of touch with our passions and instincts. The man of high character recalls the valid principles that he has discovered and continues to pursue such principles so that he can experience the greatness of these principles.

What are valid principles that we should pursue? Those that are proven to contribute to the benefit of our instincts.

By continuing to pursue valid principles, he can rekindle the flame of passion. We love that which contributes to our instincts, and therefore, we rekindle our passions when we engage in valid principles. By pursuing valid principles, despite the lack of passion, we will experience a natural reward of love and joy. This reassures man in the virtuous lifestyle of pursuing his instincts. *True belief can only be exposed when we persist despite being separated.*

True belief can only be displayed when the foundation that has shaped our lives is removed, thereby allowing us to prove our devotion to a certain lifestyle. This is why you must aim to no longer remain a child under the strict rules of your parents when you are capable of handling life on your own. This is why Jesus left earth and replaced His presence with the Holy Spirit. Perhaps an opportunity for true belief is ideal at times to confirm and refine our devotion to a certain lifestyle.

When your instincts disappear, pursue them. When your passion for the ideal vanishes, pursue it.

Some say to *follow your passions*. I disagree. Pursue the ideal; do not resort back to another passion that appears to be more fun in the moment.

Every person who has ever started a business or written a book or embarked upon a worthwhile adventure or a relationship has had passion in the beginning, and there comes a time when the passion fades away and the person wants to quit. Men of high character do not fall for their new passion of laziness. No! They persist in their meaningful goal. The greater man chooses to take control and persist for they desire to achieve something meaningful and worthwhile.

When they are tired, they keep working. When they have moments when they no longer feel attracted to their wife, they stay loyal and honorable and seek ways to rekindle it. When they are overwhelmed, they create a plan to allow them to focus and deal with the problem.

The test of a man is not what he is born into or how he allows his natural environment to move him. The test of a man is if he is willing to bear responsibility, contend with the catalysts of growth, give it his all and persist for what is truly good and beneficial. Then we can see the value of a man, which is the level to which he can exercise each virtue at the proper time.

We all should desire to be great and valuable. Often, when we are not great in one aspect, we ignore that aspect and say that richness or greatness is defined by the one aspect we excel in. But the man of high character knows that greatness is the accumulation of all virtues. Greatness is measured by how capable we are in properly utilizing wealth, strength, power, intellect, ambition, anger, love, hate, patience and courage.

Religion

We ought to be as rational as possible in pursuing our instincts. This ought to inspire us to work hard in order to get and maintain a job, to raise a family with love and to aim to preserve and better ourselves. To spend valuable time pursuing something that does not contribute to our instincts is immoral when it takes the time away from pursuing our true instincts. Therefore, we ought to ask ourselves: should we pursue a religion?

Karl Marx said that religion is the "opium of the people"[21]—and he is right. The religious get some natural instinctual reward, a high so to speak, in their pursuit of religion. It is like when you work out, and your body releases serotonin as a reward as you are working on yourself and engaging with the instinct of attempting to become great. It's like when you accomplish a project and get a feeling of satisfaction and pride. We were designed to do these beneficial things, and happiness is the reward to keep us going along that path.

To be clear, just because you feel happiness does not mean you are on the right path. For example, you might receive a high from working out even when your workout is dangerous and avoids all the muscles that you should be engaging for your sport. The natural high means that you are interacting with instincts—even if you go about it irrationally. Those who lack rationality will only hurt themselves in the long run.

Perhaps Marx proved that we should pursue a god because it seems that *pursuing a commitment to the greatest thing is a natural instinct*; we need only to find the right way of exercising this instinct. That does not mean we throw out all that relates to our instincts. We should not denounce exercising because some get hurt. We should not hate all medicine because some drugs destroy lives.

The involvement in a religion does illicit a natural response that, I believe, confirms our human instinct to pursue God. Therefore, if you have this belief instinct, then pursue it. When you have your instinctual goal set up, such as finding God, then go about it as rationally as you can.

Some, who have this belief instinct, say that they believe in a *divine being* but do not know what it is. Fair enough. How do you know which religion is right? How can you be rational in your pursuit? Just because you are of a certain religion and experience a miracle, how can you know that it was your god and not the god of another religion who just granted you mercy or grace?

I would start here: learn proper philosophy and see if any divine being is in accordance with proper philosophy. For if any religion teaches us to be against the very essence of humanity, then how could that religion's god be the divine creator that gave us such instincts? Therefore, learn proper philosophy and the proper path in life that we should all embark upon. Learn what teaches us to grow and become an individual and use your conscience and pursue your God-given instincts! That is the proper path.

Most religions do not teach the proper path. Islam, for example, requires strict obedience to rules and acts as a tyrant, not cultivating virtuous people and giving them freedom to best pursue their instincts.

Most religions still hold on to an earthly leader who dictates the lives of its followers or tells them what rules they must follow, instead of encouraging them to think for themselves. Very few religions preach the idea of becoming independent and using your conscience to take on responsibility and live to your full potential.

Perhaps I have yet to explore all religions—but it seems to me that the Protestant version of Christianity is the only religion that I have come across that allows for a proper philosophy. I am not saying that it is properly taught by most Protestant preachers, as I think many are still legalistic in their teachings and follow the rules blindly like sheep and do not use their conscience. But if you follow the actual ideas of the Christian Bible and what Jesus taught, I do believe that Protestantism does align with proper philosophy that encourages people to liberate themselves from strict rules and to transcend into being individuals who achieve great things because they have the freedom to pursue what they see as ideal.

If you do believe there is some divine being out there, explore the options and cling to the one that teaches you to move along the proper path.

And I have no doubt that many religions can be circumstantially helpful for some people. Some religions may even be great in some aspects. But as Nietzsche said:

"Whatever liberates even out of the deepest need, the rarest, the most difficult-that they call holy.
Whatever makes them rule and triumph and shine, to the awe and envy of their neighbors, that is to them the high, the first, the meaning of all things." [22]

CHAPTER 9

"God, grant me the serenity to accept the things I cannot change,
Courage to change the things I can,
And wisdom to know the difference."
- The Serenity Prayer, made popular by Dr. Reinhold Niebuhr[1]

The Pursuit of Happiness

Freedom and Loyalty

The aim of this chapter is not to convince you to join a certain political group. It is to draw the lines clearly in stone that determine when a political movement goes too far and should not be supported. We are often able to tell that a movement had gone too far in hindsight, but what can we look for in the present and the future? We tend to be sensitive to the opposing party when we believe they cross the line, yet we rarely consider where the line may lie for our own party.

After we dive into the bounds of where politics lay, we will then explore the bounds that an individual should abide within their own personal philosophy.

INDIVIDUAL FREEDOM

I have said that we should try to understand and utilize the tools (virtues) we have available, but is this applicable to everything? Should the government try to control everything the best they can and play with economic levers and move the society in ways that the elected see as ideal?

There are times when individual liberties are in conflict with the government's liberty to act. In such cases, we generally believe that the individual ought to have the right to act as they please, unless the individuals chooses to relinquish their responsibility to the government or someone else. The United States was founded upon the idea that we would rather give the power to the individual than the collective group. Why? Because we know that it is better for everyone to have a chance to be virtuous rather than a few lawmakers to have a chance to be virtuous. It is better for each individual to be conscious and choose to be righteous when they are capable of doing so, rather than blindly following the rules of a few national leaders.

Sure, a few lawmakers might do a better job at choosing what is right in many circumstances. But would you rather be a robot at the whim of someone else or would you prefer to have the freedom to think for yourself and use your conscience? I would prefer to be a human. I think it is proper to allow individuals to become capable and virtuous and grant them the freedom to think for themselves. But I must say—there is a time for each season.

TWO QUESTIONS

Let me begin by asking two questions:

First question: Is it better to have a good and wise tyrannical leader with unwise citizens or a complete freedom in a society of unwise citizens? Stop. Don't just opt for the latter because it sounds like the right answer. Think about it. If you are a parent to five young children, do you let them decide on where they go to dinner? Or do you (the good authoritarian leader) choose what your children are eating? *Answer:* It is better to have a good and wise tyrannical leader (meaning that the leader has full control of other's actions) when you have unwise people that you are responsible for just as it is best for a parent to rule over his children until the children are able to handle responsibilities.

Second question: Is it better to have a good and wise tyrannical leader with wise citizens or wise citizens with the freedom to choose for themselves? *Answer:* It is better to have a group of wise citizens with freedom. Once you are wise and virtuous and capable of handling yourself, you no longer need a tyrant ruling your life and ought to be granted freedom. We should not aim to have a parent over us making the decisions for us forever. No! We ought to pursue a state where the people are virtuous and are able to pursue what is most meaningful in their lives without an authoritarian telling them what to do.

This is not to tell you to find someone smarter than all the rest and allow him to be a tyrant; it is to say that when citizens are capable of making decisions without chaos ensuing, then let them. Let each individual live their own life and let them make their own decisions when they are capable. Let them experiment with the great challenges they wish to bear and become strong and wiser in their freedom. Give them the opportunity to reach their potential.

UNWISE CHILDREN

What would happen if five young children were given complete control of their own lives? If you sprung this freedom on them one day, then the children would indulge in the luxuries from which they have been restrained. They would eat pizza and play video games all day long. They would stay up late and become fat and avoid any responsibilities. But what would happen after a month? Most of the children would get sick; they would hate their circumstances and the unhealthy food that they have overindulged in. They would desire for a parent to step back into the parenting role and provide some stability in their lives because they themselves would know that their way of life was not ideal.

The children might not know what the parent does that makes the parent wise, but they know that the parent is wise enough to get them out of their miserable condition. So the parent, following the children's wishes, would step back in as the tyrant who makes the rules for the kids. But the story does not end here. The kids would enjoy their healthy foods and good health for a moment, but then complain of the restrictions that they have. They will say they want freedom to make their own decisions because there are times that the parental restrictions will conflict with their interests.

So as the children gradually get more uncomfortable with their lack of freedom, they will vote out the tyrant and go back to their unrestricted freedom. And the cycle repeats.

One of three things may stop this cycle.

First, the children's freedom can potentially lead to them doing something so dangerous that they end their own lives. Second, the parent decides to stop giving into the children's changing demands and chooses to permanently cement themselves as the tyrant or as the parent without any control. This would result in either a tyrannical parent who makes all the decisions for the children forever or a parent who allows their children to do whatever they please even though they are often incapable of making wise decisions. Third, the children can become virtuous. If the children are taught to utilize their own understanding and actually learn what foods and actions are healthy and the importance of them, then the children will be able to survive and live well without the need of the parents as the tyrant.

Obviously, the third option is ideal. Therefore, we must always aim to teach our children to be virtuous, to aim for what is ideal and become capable of handling responsibilities.

Aim to be capable of handling freedom; that way, you may be deserving of it.

Unwise Citizens

The same story could be said for the citizens of a nation.

If we have citizens who do not pursue virtuousness and the ideal, then we will want a wise tyrant to create order so that society can function and not fall into overwhelming chaos because we are unwise. And if the tyrant forces a strict set of virtues and culture, then after the chaos becomes order, we will revolt and scream for the opportunity to grow up and become individuals who should be allowed to think for themselves. If we rebel against the established culture and norms *without any aim at what is ideal*, then things will turn into overwhelming chaos, and the cycle will repeat. But if we rebel against the culture and norms by *aiming at what we see as ideal*, then they will create a better place and a stable society where we have virtuous citizens who have freedom.

The only way to stop the swing between overwhelming chaos and overwhelming order is by teaching citizens to properly handle freedom. If we do not encourage people to be virtuous, we sacrifice the ideal political structure.

Let me break it down by explaining how we react to a war. In war, particularly an invasion by a foreign country, we are in a state of overwhelming chaos. We are in a state where individuals are not currently able to defend themselves and survive an invasion if we do not all work together. In a sense, we are not virtuous enough to handle the burden of defending ourselves individually. We are children who will die if we do not go back to our parents for help. So we move back in with our parents and live under their rules until we are safe to go back out. We give more power back to the wise tyrant who can create a state where we will survive. We say that the president has the power to lead us into war and be the chief (Commander in Chief or the Supreme Commander of the military).

However, and this is important, the people must choose to give the tyrant his power. Congress, being the representative of the people, must declare war, and in effect, hand the president the power to temporarily be a dictator in war matters. The president then has the power to direct large groups of men and make decisions for the group as a whole.

We should not have an *absolute* aim to give responsibility back to the authority. We should only do it when not doing it will lead to a state of chaos. We should have an *absolute* aim to be developed enough to handle responsibilities and the chaos that may come. But there are times when the chaos is so overwhelming that it is proper for the citizens to give up their freedom to authority so the parent can handle it best (given that the authority is wise). *Independence is also a virtue. We should not always aim to possess it, but we should aim to be capable of handling it.*

This does not give the parent or the authority the right to take away others' freedom; it merely says that there may come a time when the citizens should give up their freedoms to the authority. It is very rare but examples of such times are during declared wars and during a national emergency.

I believe it was good for God to be a tyrant over the people of Israel in the Old Testament when they were in a stage of building themselves into a great nation. He was a good God, and He released the responsibility of authority from Himself and His strict rules and gave it to the people when they were capable of handling the responsibility.

So, to create the ideal state, we must do three things. First, teach virtues properly, as I have attempted to do in this book. Teach them to be capable of great strength, great intellect, great love and great anger; and teach them the proper times to utilize each virtue. Second, give citizens freedom and allow the citizens to give the power back to a wise tyrant when they deem things to be too chaotic for them to handle. Ideally, the citizens are developed and virtuous enough that they never deem anything too chaotic. Third, when the authority is given the power, the authority should allow a path for the citizens to become virtuous enough to one day take over and manage the chaos by themselves. For example, if the government makes it illegal to compete with the government's programs of delivering mail or exploring outer space, then that would be wrong.

Freedom, forgiveness and romantic love are wonderful things! It is ideal to be in a state of such things. But sometimes, when the world is chaotic and dark, we must think and realize that it is not always proper to have freedom, forgiveness and romantic love. But we should have an absolute aim to be in the state where we can have freedom because we are developed, where we can forgive others because they are also virtuous and trustworthy and where we have a partner who understands what marriage is and loves us.

But when we are not at such points, it may be proper to give up freedoms, trust and romantic love.

This political philosophy is the same philosophy of libertarians when society is capable of handling responsibilities. However, when individuals are incapable of handling the problems without society falling into chaos, then I believe some government intervention may be necessary. When we are children in a chaotic and overwhelming state, this philosophy allows for citizens to call on a wise tyrant, which is something libertarians rarely consider to be proper.

I would consider myself to mainly be a libertarian in most

circumstances, yet also Machiavellian at times, meaning that I believe *the ends justify the means*[2], when the end is warding off chaos.

Now, please do not misunderstand me. I do not have an absolute desire for us to be in a tyrannical state. However, I understand that there are proper circumstances when a wise man will give up his freedom so the wise tyrant can properly run things when there is chaos. I am no fan of tyrants, but desperate times call for desperate measures.

However, if the only option is an evil or unwise tyrant, then I would say it is never good to put such a person in control.

BOUNDS OF PROPER POLITICS

When do conservatives go too far? When do liberals go too far? When can we say, without the advantage of hindsight, that things were taken too far?

Generally, the right goes *too far* when it keeps its constituents in the foundational stage of life and does not give them the opportunity to transcend or when it mandates certain actions because it believes they are absolutely virtuous and *absolutely good* or it disallows certain actions because they are considered categorically bad. They might say that you must be loyal or must pray to a certain god. They might say that you cannot do something that is not generally conducive to their goal. In times of chaos, it may be acceptable to mandate certain rules to keep order. But in times of peace, the right goes too far by being the tyrant.

Generally, the left goes *too far* when it wants to tumble the pillars of society because it *wants to change* without regard for what is actually ideal. This is the result of a group that sees the foundational stage of life as unnecessary and loses its aim or purpose. The far-left is so afraid that culture will be mandated that they hate the largest cultures that are the most threatening, even if those cultures are generally good and provide good principles or aims.

Thomas Szasz writes in *The Second Sin* that "*Language separates men from other animals. It also reduces them to the level of animals—as in calling Jews 'vermin' or policeman 'pigs.'*"[3] Speaking can bring some up while tearing others down. But that does not mean that we are to remove the freedom of speech (the established culture), so that some are not labeled animals, for then surely, we will all become no different than animals.

Both the left and the right have legitimate concerns but can overcompensate to keep their worst fears from materializing. It makes sense that liberals want change. *Change* is important to life as it provides purpose and results in an awakening of the *consciousness.* It makes sense that conservatives want to hold on to the past. *History* is useful in understanding past actions so that we can analyze them and utilize what has worked the best, resulting in a process establishing *prosperous stability.* Both are necessary. Neither ought to be neglected.

A man of high character knows when to pursue *change* and when to pursue the *status quo.* He does not blindly pursue change for the sake of change, and he does not blindly pursue the past for the sake of stability. This goes for politics, forgiveness, love, business, art, philosophy and all things.

As an individual, a man of high character pursues the ideal in his own life. As a voter, he pursues freedom so that each individual can also pursue their own ideal, unless freedom would result in chaos.

RIGHTS

English philosopher John Locke favored the notion that we have *natural rights* which entitles each person to life, liberty and property.

"…no one ought to harm another in his life, health, liberty, or possessions."

- John Locke[4]

This is the idea that libertarians subscribe to. Do whatever you want, but do not impede on the natural rights of another person. We should ponder why the government needs to have an authoritarian power and enforce these specific natural rights. For if you truly wanted freedom, why not just have full liberty to do whatever you want, including lying, stealing, cheating on your spouse, murder or something else that is immoral? Why not?

Imagine a world where there are no laws at all. It is pure anarchy. You could kill me and walk away with no consequences. Perhaps people will not interact with you, but you would not get in trouble from any government. Perhaps people would kill you in response out of a preemptive attack to defend themselves. There would be no formal justice, and accusations would turn into a mob court that punished people on public opinion. There would be chaos. Pure chaos. And when a society is in pure chaos, they will resort to a tyrant to create order. For order from a wise tyrant is better than a group of crazy people with democracy. But this is not ideal.

Therefore, if we have no authority at all in our hypothetical situation, then chaos will ensue, and we will resort to authority. Therefore, we might as well set up the minimum amount of authority from the start to keep us out of a chaotic state. In order to do so, the things we must protect are life, liberty and property. If you did not protect those things, then chaos would ensue.

Think about it this way. Am I allowed to affect you? Some would say "*No*," but they actually don't mean that. The answer is both yes and no. I can bump into you accidentally on the street. I can talk to you and have my voice emit a sound wave that resonates in your eardrum and vibrates the hair cells that allow you to hear what I am saying—in effect, affecting your hair cells. I can create advertisements that convince you to buy my product. But I cannot punch you or harm you with a weapon. Why? Because we draw the line at things that cause too much chaos.

If you talk to people, you are affecting them. But it is usually a minimal amount of chaos that is manageable and will only cause a lot of chaos if you are being extremely loud to the point of hurting people's eardrums. Therefore, we generally do not mind if people affect each other when someone speaks in public.

But we draw the line at violence or restraining someone or taking property because if you affect someone by doing one of those things, then someone will retaliate, and mayhem will ensue. To live in a society where this is unrestricted would result in chaos.

We should allow some strict rules, but only when chaos would ensue without them.

And this is proper. The word "dictator" comes from Latin and was originally used by the Romans as "*a judge in the Roman republic temporarily invested with absolute power.*"[5] But it was temporary and only applied in times of war or for a specific duty that required absolute power. Julius Caesar was assassinated by his own senate, less than two months after Caesar obtained the title of *Dictator Perpetuo* (dictator in perpetuity).[6]

What we ought to say is that we should have the right to an authoritarian government that only acts in times when extreme chaos is probable. Otherwise, we should aim to be free. This means that the government would protect each and every citizen's life, liberty and property *except when the government needs to impede on these rights in order to prevent an extreme amount of chaos.* You could call such rights *proper rights.*

Therefore, the government should protect life, liberty and property, as these things will always need protecting from the government to establish some level of order. However, there are some exceptions to these rules. The exceptions, again, are to prevent an extreme amount of chaos.

The government should have the right to take away your life when you have killed other people and are likely to create more chaos the next time you are let out of jail. Obviously, the ideal is that we have virtuous men who do not murder the innocent. But if we do have murderous men, then it would be acceptable to have capital punishment or keep them in jail forever to prevent extreme chaos by letting them go free.

The government should have the right to take away your property if you have not paid the money you owe to another person. Obviously, the ideal is that we have virtuous citizens who honor their agreements. But if we do not have honorable citizens, then it is acceptable for the government to take it by force and give it to its rightful owner so that there can be some level of trust in the society.

The government should have the right to set up a draft to choose men to defend the nation when no men volunteer (or get paid to fight). Obviously, the ideal is that we have virtuous men who stand up and willingly fight for what they believe in, and luckily, we do. But if we did not, then it would be acceptable to have a draft in order to protect our country.

The government should have the right to set up borders. Obviously, the ideal is that we have virtuous immigrants who are beneficial to our society, and we let everyone in. But as we know that some may not desire to contribute to our society, it is acceptable to have a border and vetting process to try to weed out the individuals who are likely to cause chaos.

And perhaps this argument could be applied to welfare. If the poorest of the poor were revolting because they had no safety net and were about to riot and cause chaos, which has happened many times before, then it is reasonable to make sure that there is a system that has taxes to prevent the extreme chaos. Obviously, the ideal is that individuals take care of themselves, and we are charitable when they are unable to pay for themselves. But if we are not charitable, then it would be acceptable to have the lowest amount of taxes to prevent the extreme chaos of a revolt. If not that, then you would have to raise an army to stop them which would also be a cost. Pick your poison. But it seems that a safety net is usually more ideal for everyone, including the rich and the poor.

You must have a consistent philosophy, and if you base it on the prevention of chaos to prevent full authoritarianism, then taxation for jails, courts, army and welfare may be proper to prevent chaos when citizens are not virtuous.

Established rights are not meant to stop or defuse all chaos, but only the extreme chaos that has the potential to destroy or seriously wound a society. And in order to prevent the chaos, sometimes, the government will have to step in and prevent the chaos. In such times and such times only, the ends (preventing chaos) justify the means (the minimum amount of taxation).

There are no inherent human rights. Not life, liberty, property, healthcare, food, roads, education or anything. If there were human rights, then how could someone kill you or take your liberty and put you in chains? You are not guaranteed anything just because you are a human.

But some things are so essential to a properly functioning society that if we do not create legislation around them, then extreme chaos will ensue. Therefore, any civilized society must create laws that protect life, liberty and the property. Rights and regulations are only guaranteed insofar as a governing body can enforce its laws.

Do not end the debate by saying something should be a right because you want it. Do not say the government should ban something because you dislike it or think it is wrong. Prove that, without such legislation, extreme chaos will ensue. Otherwise, allow for liberty.

God gave us all that we have, but He does not ensure that we get to keep it. It is up to us to create a society that allows us to function best and be good stewards of that which we are given in life.

Until we are all truly virtuous and aim to not harm each other, until we are all civilized and generous enough to not require a welfare system, until we are trustworthy enough to not need government, then we shall need some form of government to institute some level of order.

A society is only capable of properly bearing as much freedom as it is virtuous.

Independence and freedom are virtues. They are good ideals when we are virtuous and capable. But currently, as we are not virtuous enough, we must have some level of authoritarianism and a reduced level of freedom. But we should always strive to be able to earn more freedom, and we should always grant the individual as much freedom as they are capable of handling.

RIGHTS AND RESPONSIBILITIES

"I believe that every right implies a responsibility."

- John D. Rockefeller, Jr.[7]

We ought to be careful when we declare certain desires to be our right because when we legally institute a right, we also are forcing a responsibility. Legal rights require others to bear responsibilities, regardless of whether they want to bear that responsibility or not. There are occasions when rights are good and necessary, but these are rare, and we should highly scrutinize anyone shouting for more rights. For every right that is given, the state requires everyone else to be responsible to honor that right.

If someone wants the right to free healthcare, for instance, then taxpaying citizens have the responsibility to pay for it. If you want the right to vote, the government has the responsibility to allow you to vote without impeding your ability to vote.

We love to get rights, but we hate giving other people rights because then we are left with new responsibilities that not everyone is on board with. When we demand a right, we demand that others give up their freedom and honor the right we demand.

For example, we ought to consider if we want law enforcement to have the right to enforce the law. Most, including myself, like the idea of giving law enforcement that right so that we do not fall into a state of chaos. If we give them that right, all citizens have the *responsibility* to honor and respect them when they are working. Yet, the same groups that shout that they want more rights do not take a moment to consider that they should start shouting for us to be responsible for the rights we have already established. They have only known the idea of establishing new rights, not of the burden that each right implies. They think that if you establish a right, then the world will automatically be transformed into a place of happiness and peace. But in reality, it means forcing responsibility on others. The individual is not given the opportunity to choose the most meaningful responsibility in their life but is prescribed a certain responsibility that very well may be less meaningful to them. It means sacrificing freedom to choose the ideal. The only time we should sacrifice such freedom is to prevent a state of chaos.

How to Deal with Chaos

Become strong enough and capable enough to deal with chaos by yourself. But sometimes, chaos is too overwhelming for an individual. And in such times, it is ideal to work with a group to solve the problem. Sometimes we need John the Baptist to help us out of the chaos when it weighs us down. Sometimes we need a spotter when weightlifting to help us when we struggle against the heavy weight above our body.

In theory, healthcare insurance companies are a prime example. They invite people who want to pool their money together. When something becomes too overwhelming for one person, they help out the person who is in overwhelming chaos. Though everyone pays into it, people with expensive procedures that they could not handle by themselves (extreme chaos) get help.

They are there for a chaotic time when an individual is not capable of handling the burden of medical costs, which is good because sometimes, healthcare costs can be so overwhelming that we need to have the option to call on an insurance company to cover the crazy costs of healthcare when we cannot afford them.[8]

In life, it is good to be prepared. To be in a place so close to chaos, where one moment can ruin your life, is risky and may force you to continually do things that are not ideal. Therefore, try to safeguard against anything that may potentially cause extreme chaos.

In short, when a necessary task is too much for an individual to handle, they are better off partnering with others so that their combined efforts, or authoritative and wise leadership, can help them accomplish the necessary task.

For example, when we are at war, we should all become one and under the direction of the wise leader of our country and allow him to make the rules.

When we are at risk of being unable to pay for catastrophic costs like healthcare, we should group together with other individuals and cover ourselves with insurance, so it does not ruin our lives.

When we need to pursue our instinct of reproducing and cannot do it by ourselves, let us group with another so that we can, thereby becoming one. To reproduce is to continue a part of yourself into the future and to not have your essence come to an end. And in order to go about this instinct to reproduce rationally so that your offspring have the best chance of survival and also have their own offspring, then perhaps marriage is the most rational way of doing so.

Loyalty should be extended only towards a trustworthy person or an entity whom you need to ward off chaos. Otherwise, pursue individuality so you are most free to decide how to live righteously.

This is not to be confused with the accepting of others as we see in *agapē* when you trust someone. We should only sacrifice our individuality and freedom when we absolutely must. We ought to welcome others into our lives with friendship when we trust.

THE IDEAL MINDSET IN THE NON-CHAOTIC STATE

Do not be so far to the right that you limit humans to do what has been done in the past and has been the initial inspiration and guide. Allow people to think and aim as they please. Perhaps they will find an even better way of life. You ought to aim to maximize your rationality.

Do not be so far to the left that you try to kill people's natural guide and instincts. Let them strive for greatness and be better than others as they engage with their innate desires. Do not hammer out children's instincts by indoctrinating them to think that their efforts for greatness are meaningless. Do not be so far to the left that you kill instincts and the natural guides that people need to find meaning in life. You ought to aim to maximize your love for your instincts.

Do not be so far to the right that you preach the idea that fitting in is the absolute ideal as an attempt to kill the individual's instinct for greatness. Do not be so far to the left that you preach always standing apart from the norm. Be wise. Stick with the norms and the culture; but when you discover something that differs from the norm that is worth attaining and that you are capable of attaining, then stand apart and chase it, which is why *the truth* is so valuable. If we do not know the true value of the options, then how will we ever know when to deviate from the past and pursue something greater? Discovering the truth allows us to properly make decisions in aiming at virtuousness.

Do not tell me that I cannot judge or that I should not have the right to be disgusted because everything is meaningless and has equal value. Do not be so far left that you say that it does not matter which virtue you choose for any given circumstance, for there is no ideal way to act.

I am saying that you should aim for what makes you stronger and greater; otherwise, you will stay in stagnation or decay and both of those will eventually lead to death. The phrase *"what does not kill you makes you stronger"*[9] is not exactly right (nor do I think Nietzsche thought it was always right when he wrote it despite the fact that he is attributed the phrase). What we ought to say is, *"what does not make you stronger, kills you."* [10]

So do not go too far to the left and tell me I cannot be disgusted or that I cannot have an ideal and express it. Do not tell me that the *ideal human* should not have an ideal to aim at and that I should aim to be your version of the *ideal human*.

Do not go too far to the right and tell others that they must behave a certain way that you see as ideal and consider to be an absolute ideal. Allow others the freedom to explore and possibly discover a new way to grow. Do not say that you have determined what the ideal is and that I must forgo determining what the ideal is so that I can blindly obey your ideal.

Both political parties are at risk of destroying society. The right can prevent us from being virtuous by disallowing us to think about what is actually ideal and forcing us to do what is generally considered the absolute ideal. The left can disallow us to think about what is truly ideal by removing the ability to have an ideal.

Neither are transcendent at the extremes. Neither are virtuous at the extremes. To be virtuous is to consciously determine which available target is the best and to aim for that ideal in the best way that you are capable of.

AUTHORITARIANISM IN A NON-CHAOTIC STATE

Why does this book matter? Because we continue to promote authoritarian ideas when we are in a non-chaotic state. Because we see some virtues as always good and others as always bad, and we do not know how to properly teach virtues. Because most say that authoritarianism is always bad, but some can come up with a few examples of when it is good, so authoritarian supporters promote it at all times. We still like to see things in black and white.

The only time the government should be involved is when the people are unable to provide the need themselves and the need is truly a need. For example, we needed the government to create roads and deliver mail when the country first began because no business was capable of doing such a task. But as we evolved as a nation and businesses have become capable of handling large tasks, we ought to release the responsibility from the government to the individuals when the individuals are capable of handling it.

Perhaps we are like children in some regards and cannot handle every task yet. There may be times when we need to pool our money together and have the government run it and set roles as if they were our parents. There are times when the free market is not developed enough to sustain the needed projects.

But our goal should be to develop ourselves to the point where we can handle projects and then remove the responsibility from the parent and give it to the children when they are developed enough to handle it. That's what a good parent does.

Obviously, there is an ultimate political ideal, and it is not authoritarian, but we must think rationally and as a man of high character would—one who does not see the world in black and white but uses his conscience.

The right goes too far when it forces virtues in times that are not chaotic. They say to always be courageous and kind and clean. When cleanliness is considered an absolutely good virtue, then some will do whatever it takes to be clean regardless of the circumstances. For example, Adolf Hitler was highly sensitive to filth and wanted everything to be clean. So what does a clean freak do in order to follow the virtue of cleanliness? Wipe out the filth. He often took several baths in a single day for his own personal hygiene.[11] He also referred to the Jews as filth, rats and parasites and tried to cleanse them from Germany. Hitler wanted a perfectly clean world! It was black and white for him, and he thought that he should always pursue cleanliness, regardless of circumstances.

Hitler started with those he saw as most filthy. In his opinion, the Jews were the filthiest, then the homosexuals, then those who disagreed with his politics, then people of other races and the list goes on. He had no understanding of the proper time to clean and the proper time to allow imperfect humans to exist.

Tyrannical leaders kill the humanity within people by not allowing people to be virtuous and think for themselves about what a man of high character ought to do; therefore, such leaders should only be allowed temporarily when tyranny is necessary for humanity to survive.

The authoritarian state hinders our ability to be properly virtuous. It tells us exactly what to do and does not ask us to use our conscience. It creates broad rules that are not ideal for every situation. It should only be used in times of dire chaos so that we can survive and then take our freedom back when we are no longer in dire chaos.

I do worry that the liberal's pursuit of change may take place in the wrong area. For example, a liberal may want *the government to change* and to establish new laws. What they should do is aim for the government to allow freedom so that *individuals have the opportunity to change*.

And I worry about the conservatives, for sometimes they want the government to restrict freedom so that *people do not change*. What they should do is aim for the government to allow freedom so that individuals can *best decide how to live* their own lives.

WHY WE DIFFER (THE BEGINNING OF AN INDIVIDUAL'S PHILOSOPHICAL BOUNDS)

Conservatives want us to have a universal culture that allows us to trust each other, so they lean towards shaping the culture in ways they see as ideal. They want to have words properly defined so that we can communicate. They want people to behave a certain way so that we have a functional community. They want everyone to have a proper aim of living, to prosper and care for their children.

Conservatives favor stability, for it is tested and proven.

Liberals fear that such an idea of a universal culture may require certain ideals or certain perspectives that may be incorrect. Liberals believe that most people have the potential to be more virtuous than the basic culture, so they often attack culture to make it easier for people to think for themselves instead of just relying on the culture. When conservatives only cling to the status quo and do not allow thinking for one's self about the ideal and dare to embrace that which is worthwhile, we say that such a person lacks individuality. They cower from the task of being a good steward of their conscience.

Liberals favor change, for through change, we often experience consciousness and adventure.

We should choose to engage in change when we do it with the purpose of creating something meaningful that helps us reach our ideal. That is the idea of transcending. To shy away from transcending is to be too conservative. To engage in chaos for the sake of rebelling without aiming for an ideal is too chaotic and too liberal.

We should aim for change and rebellion and revolution when we are aimed at something better. Do not rebel and change the norms and status quo when there are no better options. Do not ask for change and destroy the norms unless you have a solution to make things better. The only exception to this is when things are so terrible under the current norms that you must free yourself in hopes of stumbling across something better. This is much riskier, but may be ideal in desperate times.

Do not be so conservative that you stick to art that is only black and white and safe and disallow the use of other colors. Do not be so liberal that you are an artist that is random and without aim or philosophy in your art.

Do not stick to only safe virtues like courage and patience and disallow anger for yourself or for others. Do not exhibit the virtues randomly, out of rebellion or without regard for which is right.

The greater man has an aim and then uses whichever tools, colors or virtues available to best articulate his aim.

Conservatives tend to admire rules and norms but go too far when they forget that the goal should be to transcend the strict rules and to think for ourselves. Liberals tend to admire the idea of getting rid of the rules completely but go too far when they forget that you must have some norms and consensual pursuits (furthering instincts) so that liberty is not completely chaotic and freedom can be properly aimed at pursuing righteousness.

We ought to be able to say something is moral or immoral and we ought to be able to shame or hate that which teaches nihilism. However, we ought to allow people the freedom to speak freely and against the established norms.

Liberals are right to be concerned that norms and virtues should not always be forced, for loyalty is not always good when you are following an evil tyrant. And conservatives are right that trust and norms are needed for a society to function.

Conservatives are more likely to trust the current state of affairs and find the risk of deviating to be costly. Liberals tend to distrust the current state of affairs and find the risk of deviating to be minimal and the reward to be worthwhile.

AIM FOR THE IDEAL

Do not shed your ways until you find something better. Perhaps doing nothing is better than your current ways, and you should shed your old ways for nothing, but do not shed the old ways for the sake of change. Shed your old ways only when you have good reason to do so.

Being conservative is trusting that the present norms are the current ideal. Being liberal is trusting the risk of the future change is ideal. (These characterizations do not strictly correspond to any political party's platform.)

Liberals, do not be afraid to hold on to that which is great when there is nothing better to aim for. Conservatives, do not be afraid to reach for new heights when you have comfort and order in the moment and when there is something better to aim for.

The conservative goes too far when they only act on fear and refuse to allow something that is worthwhile. The liberal goes too far when they only act on imagination and do not consider the reality of problems that such changes will bring. The greater man is the one who seriously considers the risks of change while also imagining and striving for the ideal.

Do not shave your head solely for the purpose of being different and then call yourself brave. Yet, many think being different is inherently inspiring and beautiful. It is not, unless you are pursuing something more beautiful or worthwhile. Do not be a rebel without a cause. Be a rebel when you have a cause and fit in when you lack a worthwhile cause.

Do not be so liberal that you desire *change* and *progress* without concern for what change and progress may result in. Be wise and pursue change when it is worthwhile and be content when things are working well and there is nothing worth changing for. Make the calculations and determine if change is worth the cost. If it is worthwhile, only then should the individual do it.

Do not be so conservative that you look at the past and only attempt to emulate the past actions as if they are undoubtedly ideal. Perhaps the ideal has yet to be discovered. Do not be so liberal that you run from the ideal when you stumble across it. Perhaps the ideal has been discovered.

Do not be so conservative that you want the past ways to remain that you will eradicate or disallow those who bring worthwhile change.

Do not be so conservative that you will not give up the good to go for the great. And do not be so liberal that you disregard what is great and only pursue change.

To be too conservative is to never ask yourself, "*What do I actually want?*" and only consider the options you know. To be too liberal is to only ask yourself, "*What can I obtain?*" and neglect the search for the ideal or consider the limitations.

Do not be so liberal that you forget to aim for greatness and instead aim for a social cause. Do not aim for diversity in all things for that is often not the ideal. Great sport teams do not aim for equal men and women; they aim to gather the greatest players regardless of how they were born. Sometimes, diversity can be the ideal for it can introduce novel perspectives; sometimes, it limits the ability to gather the greatest contributors. Pursue the ideal, not the social cause.

Do not be so conservative that you say "*if it ain't broke, don't fix it*" to all things. Be at peace with routines and patterns when they are working well but also be willing to engage with new things when they are worthwhile.

The proper path in life calls us to not only appropriate the ideal that others have discovered but to also pursue novelty when we believe a greater ideal exists. To be too liberal is to say that we should never appropriate another's ideal but instead always create our own way. To be too conservative is to only appropriate another's ideal and never be the one to innovate.

To be too liberal is to always be an agent of chaos, pursuing change without regard for righteousness. To be too conservative is to always be an agent of order, purely devoted to maintaining the current order and being uncommitted to pursuing righteousness. Neither are for Christians nor great men, who should be slaves to righteousness.

THE PURSUIT OF HAPPINESS

I always thought that it was strange that the Declaration of Independence says we have the right to *life, liberty and the pursuit of happiness*. Where did *happiness* get introduced into all of this? Shouldn't it have said *property*? Happiness has often thought to be a feeble pursuit by the wise. Happiness has often been considered the byproduct of another, more righteous, aim.

Did Jefferson declare that our nation was founded upon the pursuit of happiness? Did we declare independence, fight an uphill battle against the English and begin our nation because we wanted to chase something we never should have aimed at? No. We have only recently misunderstood the meaning behind Jefferson's famous words "*the pursuit of happiness*."

When the word *pursuit* was used, it meant something different than how we often use it today. Harvard professor and distinguished historian Arthur Schlesinger, Sr., wrote *The Lost Meaning of 'The Pursuit of Happiness'*, in which he notes that as early as the 16th century, the word *pursuit* had two possible meanings. Schlesinger states that evidence indicates that in this context, *pursuit* meant "*practicing rather than the quest for happiness*."[12] In the same way that we "*refer to the pursuit of law or the pursuit of medicine*,"[13] we ought to think of pursuit as a lifestyle. It was not about trying to be happy, but it was about doing the things each day that brought about *happiness*.

Furthermore, we must ask what Jefferson meant by the word *happiness*. Jefferson was a scholar of the past philosophers and often used words in the same manner that philosophers did; however, the words may mean something different today. In 2015, Carli N. Conklin published "*The Origins of the Pursuit of Happiness*" in the Washington University Jurisprudence Review, in which she states that "*Happiness in this sense is synonymous with the Greek concept of eudaimonia; it evokes a sense of well being or a state of flourishing that is the result of living a fit or virtuous life.*"[14] She further clarifies the use of "fit" by saying "*'Fit' refers to an ancient and medieval concept of 'rightness' or being 'rightly ordered.' In the manner used above, a human is to be 'rightly ordered' to the law of God as it pertains to humans.*"[15]

When Thomas Jefferson wrote "*the pursuit of happiness*," he meant that the people of the United States of America ought to have the right to live a lifestyle of being virtuous—a lifestyle of pursuing our instincts rationally as a man of high character would do. This is the true pursuit that we ought to be willing to die for.

We should not aim to be men forced by others to do certain actions, but men granted the freedom to choose *good actions* over bad actions. Our nation was founded on the idea that we ought to value individual liberty and have the freedom to pursue virtuousness and righteousness and only hand back our freedom for a temporary time when we see fit as a virtuous person would. We were founded on the idea that we desire the individuals to transcend and grow so that we can become a country with men of high character.

But we have lost touch with our initial foundation. We have gone from pursuing a virtuous life to pursuing artificial happiness. We have gone from believing in freedom to believing things should be free. We ponder ways to make machines into man who can think and become conscious, all the while we allow ourselves to become like machines who are told how to act. We are closer to becoming machines than machines are to becoming human. We are closer to slavery than to freedom. We are further from true happiness than ever before because we deprive ourselves of being virtuous, because we play the game that certain virtues are always good, and others are always bad.

Some call themselves liberal, but do not realize that liberal means "*of and pertaining to freedom.*" Some call themselves conservatives but do not realize that conservativism means to conserve the original idea the founding fathers deemed to be of the utmost importance— *freedom to be virtuous.*

We are a nation that was initially designed to develop men of high character, those free to rationally pursue their God-given instincts. We can still have such a nation if we encourage citizens to speak of their ideals and aim to live virtuously. Therefore, allow individual freedom when we are not at risk of extreme chaos but always preach virtues properly and learn when and how they should be properly applied. Become the type of person who is developed enough to handle the harsh realities you may encounter so that you can be virtuous, admirable and respectable. Be the one who is a light on a hill, shining down and illuminating the world so that others can properly navigate life. Devote yourself to becoming virtuous and righteous and willingly face the chaos that can be turned into order when you are capable of facing it. That is our calling—to be a man of high character.

Endnotes

Chapter 1 - Virtues

1. Shakespeare, William. *Romeo and Juliet*. Ed. Philip Weller. Hamlet Navigator. Shakespeare Navigators, Act II, scene III, Retrieved from https://shakespeare-navigators.com/romeo/T23.html
2. Online Etymology Dictionary. Retrieved from https://www.etymonline.com/word/virtue
3. All biblical verses are derived from the English Standard Version (ESV) unless otherwise noted.
4. Aristotle. *The Nicomachean Ethics of Aristotle* (Ross, William, Trans.). Pacific Publishing Studio, 2011. Book II, p. 20.
5. Riefenstahl, Leni. *Triumph Des Willens = Triumph of the Will*. Chicago: International Historic Films, 1981. Available at https://www.amazon.com/Triumph-Will-Leni-Riefenstahl/dp/B019ZZTM0Y
6. Nietzsche, Friedrich. *Thus Spoke Zarathustra* (Kaufmann, Walter, Trans.). Penguin Classics, 1982. Second Part, p. 207.
7. Shakespeare, William. *Romeo and Juliet*. Ed. Philip Weller. Hamlet Navigator. Shakespeare Navigators, Act II, scene VI, Retrieved from https://shakespeare-navigators.com/romeo/T26.html

Chapter 2 – Forgiveness and Bitterness

1. This quote has been attributed to Bernard Meltzer. It was mostly likely spoken during his radio show and not within a book. While I am unable to find the exact location of the quote, I will continue to provide the attribution to Meltzer as it is assumed that he said the quote.

2. Forgive. *Merriam-Webster Dictionary*. Retrieved at https://www.merriam-webster.com/dictionary/forgive

3. Szasz, Thomas. *The Second Sin*. New York: Garden Press, 1973. P. 51.

4. Jampolsky, G. *Love is Letting Go of Fear*. Celestial Arts, 2011. P. 115.

5. Wallace, Daniel B. "Ephesians: Introduction, Argument, and Outline." Retrieved from https://bible.org/seriespage/ephesians-introduction-argument-and-outline

6. Pope, Alexander. *An Essay on Criticism*, Part II, 1711.

7. See https://www.haaretz.com/jewish/.premium-why-jews-stopped-sacrificing-lambs-for-passover-1.5440120

8. Szasz, Thomas. *The Second Sin*. New York: Garden Press, 1973. p. 45.

9. Tolstoy, Leo. *Three Methods of Reform*. Phamphlet, 1900. Available at https://archive.org/stream/pamphletstransl00tolsgoog/pamphletstransl00tolsgoog_djvu.txt

Chapter 3 – Trust and Faith

1. This quote has been attributed to Benjamin Franklin. While I am unable to find the exact location of the quote, I will continue to provide the attribution to Franklin as it is assumed that he said the quote.

2. Nietzsche, Friedrich. *The Gay Science* (Williams, Bernard, Edit.). Cambridge University Press, 2001. Book V, section 343, p. 199.

3. This verse is according to the New International Version (NIV). While both the ESV and NIV are translated from Greek, the ESV says "It does not insist on its own way; it is not irritable or resentful". The ESV also contains a footnote that says that the Greek word that is translated into irritable means "irritable and does not count up wrongdoing". In the end, both interpretations of the Greek do include the idea of not holding wrongs against someone.

4. The Greek words that are used can be found at https://

biblehub.com/1_corinthians/13-5.htm
Assume that for all future references of the original Greek
text, they were found at https://biblehub.com

5. I have included the original Greek word *agapē* instead of
translating it to allow the readers to realize which word was
being referred to. This applies to all verses that I reference
that contain *agapē* as the word *agapē* is always translated to
'love' in the ESV and NIV.

6. Nietzsche, Friedrich. *Beyond Good and Evil* (Kaufmann,
Walter, Trans.). The Modern Library Edition, 1992. Part IV,
#125, p. 277.

7. Tesla, Nikola. *The Electric Journal*, 1986. Volume 2, Issue
3, p. 540. Retrieved from https://books.google.com/
books?id=k4vmAAAAMAAJ

Chapter 4 - Anxiety

1. Twain, Mark. *The Tragedy of Pudd'nhead Wilson: And the
Comedy Those Extraordinary Twins.* Connecticut: American
Publishing Company, 1894. P. 155. Available at https://
books.google.com/books?id=UhgmAAAAMAAJ

2. Anxiety as Saving through Faith." In *Kierkegaard's Writings,
VIII, Volume 8: Concept of Anxiety: A Simple Psychologically
Orienting Deliberation on the Dogmatic Issue of Hereditary
Sin*, edited by Thomte Reidar, by Kierkegaard Søren and
Anderson Albert B., 155-62. Princeton, New Jersey:
Princeton University Press, 1980. http://www.jstor.org/
stable/j.ctt24hrfg.10.

3. Isbell, Lynne. *Snakes as agents of evolutionary change in
primate brains. Journal of Human Evolution, Volume 51, Issue
1, July 2006.*

4. Truman, Harry. *Public Papers of the Presidents: Harry S.
Truman—1947.* United States Government Printing Office,
1963. P. 13.

5. Truman, Harry. *Memoirs.* Garden City, New York:
Doubleday, 1955. 422-423.

6. Roosevelt, Franklin. *First Inaugural Address of Franklin*

   D. Roosevelt. 1933. Retrieved at https://avalon.law.yale.
   edu/20th_century/froos1.asp

7. Anxiety as Saving through Faith." In *Kierkegaard's Writings,
   VIII, Volume 8: Concept of Anxiety: A Simple Psychologically
   Orienting Deliberation on the Dogmatic Issue of Hereditary
   Sin*, edited by Thomte Reidar, by Kierkegaard Søren and
   Anderson Albert B., 155-62. Princeton, New Jersey:
   Princeton University Press, 1980. http://www.jstor.org/
   stable/j.ctt24hrfg.10.

8. Gracian, Baltasar. *The Art of Worldly Wisdom* (Jacobs, Joseph,
   Trans.). London: Macmillan, 1904. Section cclxviii.

CHAPTER 5 – LOVE AND HATE

1. Rand, Ayn. *The Fountainhead.* The Bobbs-Merrill Company,
   1968. Part 2, section 14, p. 388.

2. Rand, Ayn. *The Phil Donahue Show.* 1979. Interview
   available at https://youtu.be/3u8Jjth81_Q Rand discusses
   her perception of Jesus 22 minutes into the video.

3. Mother Teresa of *Calcutta. Love: A Fruit Always in Season:
   Daily Meditations by Mother Teresa.* San Fransisco: Ignatius
   Press, 1987. Quote is included in the preface.

4. This quote has been used by many people over the years.
   For more information about the origin of the idea, refer to
   https://quoteinvestigator.com/2015/06/28/bicycle/

CHAPTER 6 – CONSCIOUSNESS

1. Ribot, Théodule. The Psychology of Attention. Chicago: The
   Open Court Publishing Company, 1890, p. 46. Available at
   https://archive.org/details/psychologyofatte00ribo/page/46
   Note – While this quote is often contributed to Aldous
   Huxley in his work The Art of Seeing (1942), Huxley was
   quoting Ribot.

2. Refer to story at http://www.espn.com/espn/feature/story/_/
   page/enterpriseSalts/ezekiel-elliott-clay-matthews-just-the-
   nfl-smelling-salt-users

3. Nietzsche, Friedrich. *Beyond Good and Evil* (Kaufmann,
   Walter, Trans.). The Modern Library Edition, 1992. Part II,

section 39, p. 239.

4. Nietzsche, Friedrich. *Twilight of the Idols* (Kaufmann, Walter, Trans.). Penguin Classics, 1982. P. 507.

5. Williamson AM, Feyer A. *Moderate sleep deprivation produces impairments in cognitive and motor performance equivalent to legally prescribed levels of alcohol intoxication Occupational and Environmental Medicine 2000*;57:649-655.

6. Stephens, James Fitzjames. *Liberty, Equality, Fraternity*, ed. Stuart D. Warner. Indianapolis: Liberty Fund, 1993. Available at https://oll.libertyfund.org/titles/572

CHAPTER 7 – RESPONSIBILITY

1. Shaw, Bernard. *Back to Methuselah: A Metabiological Pentateuch*. London: Constable and Co, 1921. Retrieved from http://www.gutenberg.org/files/13084/

2. See https://definitions.uslegal.com/g/good-samaritans/

3. See https://www.haaretz.com/jewish/.premium-why-jews-stopped-sacrificing-lambs-for-passover-1.5440120

4. Dostoyevsky, Fyodor. *The Brother Karamazov* (Garnett, Constance, Trans.). New York: The Lowell Press, n.d., part II, book IV, section 318, p. 202.

5. Ibid.

6. Frankl, Victor. *Man's Search for Meaning* (Lasch, Isle, Trans.). Boston: Beacon Press, 2006. Pp.97-134.

7. Graves, Robert and Patai, Raphel. *Hebrew Myths: The Book of Genesis*. Rosetta Books LLC, 1964. See chapter 2, section 3. Also see http://thebiblenet.blogspot.com/2015/11/tehom-tahamat-tiamat.html

8. Two sources for this claim.
   1) Graves, Robert and Patai, Raphel. *Hebrew Myths: The Book of Genesis*. Rosetta Books LLC, 1964. See chapter 1, section 14.
   2) Clarke, Leonard. Greek *Astronomy and Its Debt to the Babylonians*. The British Journal for the History of Science, Vol. 1, No. 1 (Jun., 1962), pp. 65- 77.

9. See https://www.ancient.eu/article/225/enuma-elish---the-

babylonian-epic-of-creation---fu/
10. See Mark 1:3-4; Mark 1:9.
11. See Matthew 3:14.
12. See Matthew 3:15 – NIV.
13. See Mark 1:11; Matthew 3:17; Luke 3:22.
14. See John 1:32; Luke 3:22; Matthew 3:16; Mark 1:10.
15. See https://www.biblestudytools.com/lexicons/greek/nas/ baptizo.html
16. See https://en.wikipedia.org/wiki/Nicander

CHAPTER 8 - TRANSCENDING

1. Nietzsche, Friedrich. *Thus Spoke Zarathrustra* (Kaufmann, Walter, Trans.). Penguin Classics, 1982. First Part, p. 170.
2. See Genesis 22:1-18.
3. Nietzsche, Friedrich. *Thus Spoke Zarathrustra* (Kaufmann, Walter, Trans.). Penguin Classics, 1982. First Part, p. 190.
4. Luther, Martin. Final portion of his Speech at the Imperial Diet in Worms. 1521. Section 11. See https://www.bartleby.com/268/7/8.html
5. Calvin, John. *Institutes of the Christian Religion*. Book III, Chapter 19, Section 15. See https://www.biblestudytools.com/history/calvin-institutes-christianity/book3/chapter-19.html
6. Descartes, René. *Discourse on Methods* (Haldane, Elizabeth, Trans.). Digireads.com Publishing, 2016. Part IV, p. 34.
7. Nietzsche, Friedrich. *The Antichrist* (Kaufmann, Walter, Trans.). Penguin Classics, 1982. Section 3, p. 571.
8. Ibid, section 5.
9. Nietzsche, Friedrich. *The Gay Science: Book V* (Williams, Bernard, Edit.). Section 343. Cambridge University Press, 2001. P. 199.
10. Ibid.
11. Ibid.
12. Nietzsche, Friedrich. *The Antichrist* (Kaufmann, Walter, Trans.). Penguin Classics, 1982. Section 51, p. 632.
13. Ibid, section 6, p. 572.

14. Ibid, section 16, p. 583.
15. Ibid, section 25, p. 594.
16. Ibid, section 16, p. 583.
17. Ibid, section 7, p. 572-573.
18. See Joshua 2.
19. Gracián, Baltasar. *The Art of Worldly Wisdom* (Jacobs, Joseph, Trans.). London and New York: Macmillan & Co, 1892. Section 183.
20. Aurelius , Marcus. *Meditations* (Long, George, Trans.; Kaufman, William, ed.). Mineola: Dover Publications, 1997. Book 5, section 16, p. 33.
21. Marx, Karl. *Critique of Hegel's Philosophy of Right* (Jolin, Annette and O'Malley, Joseph, Trans.). Cambridge University Press, 1970. Introduction. Retrieved from https://www.marxists.org/archive/marx/works/1843/critique-hpr/intro.htm
22. Nietzsche, Friedrich. *Thus Spoke Zarathrustra* (Kaufmann, Walter, Trans.). Penguin Classics, 1982. First Part, p. 170.

CHAPTER 9 – FREEDOM AND LOYALTY

1. The serenity prayer is often attributed to Dr. Reinhold Niebuhr. A very similarly worded prayer called the "General's Prayer" from the 14th century could also be the original source. See https://www.aa.org/assets/en_US/smf-129_en.pdf
2. While Machiavelli is often quoted as saying "the ends justify the means," he never explicitly stated that phrase. However, the idea that the ends justifies the means is prevalent throughout his book *The Prince*. Machiavelli often says that a goal of a prince is to avoid being hated, because then a prince would often lose his throne as the people have the power to rebel. While *The Prince* focuses on avoiding hatred in order to retain order underneath him, I believe a more applicable approach to today's society would be to focus on avoiding overwhelming chaos in order to retain some order and structure in society.
3. Szasz, Thomas. *The Second Sin*. New York: Garden Press,

1973. P. 20.
4. Locke, John. *The Two Treatises of Civil Government*. London: Printed for Thomas Tegg; W. Sharpe and Son; G. Offor; G. and J. Robinson; J. Evans and Co.: Also R. Griffin and Co. Glasgow; and J. Gumming, Dublin, 1823. P. 107. See http://www.yorku.ca/comninel/courses/3025pdf/Locke.pdf
5. Online Etymology Dictionary. Retrieved from https://www.etymonline.com/word/dictator
6. See http://www.csun.edu/~hcfll004/datesjc.html
7. Rockefeller, John. From The Credo of John D. Rockefeller Jr. See https://library.brown.edu/create/rock50/the-credo-of-john-d-rockefeller-jr/
8. The hospital system is slightly more complicated than presented. Hospitals have set up a system that encourage you to get insurance for everything, not just the overwhelming chaos of the expensive procedures. They have jacked up the gross prices of procedures to two, three or four times the reasonable price and discount it down only for those who have submitted to the authority of the third party payer (such as an insurance company or Medicare) to negotiate a fair price on your behalf.

The hospitals say that you will only get a competitive price if you submit to a third party payer first. Otherwise, the hospital will price gouge you for being an individual. Our healthcare system has become a terrible tyrant who wants to keep you dependent and punish those who do not rely on a middle man.

I do not mean that we need the government to completely take over healthcare because there are other less intrusive ways to solve the healthcare problem. If we disallowed discounts (specifically contractual allowance), then the problem would solve itself, and we would have transparency and competition in the healthcare market so that the individual can choose an insurance company or be on his own and survive with reasonable prices.

Individuals would get the option to be on their own and pay fair prices (which would now be a third of the current price), choose almost any hospital and get a competitive rate (as now all hospitals offer everyone the reasonable rate and not just some insurance plans that they create a contract with), actually be able to see the prices (as there is no discount applied and the final price would be clear) and only need insurance in times of drastic overwhelming chaos. But currently, with contractual allowance being used by virtually all hospitals, the individual is punished by the hospital for being an individual.

9. Nietzsche, Friedrich. *Twilight of the Idols* (Kaufmann, Walter, Trans.). Penguin Classics, 1982. Maxims and Arrows #8, p. 467. I have used the most common usage of the phrase in the chapter, however, the first time it was used in the Twilight of the Idols it says: *"Out of life's school of war: What does not destroy me, makes me stronger."* In this section of his book, Nietzsche spends time trying to question the basic assumptions of society. The fact that he is stating this here is not his approval that this idea is his philosophy, and should probably be interpreted as a mockery of the idea how soldiers are willing to risk their lives for others' causes if you provide them a phrase that is sometimes accurate.

10. Marianas Trench. "Astoria." Astoria. Songwriter Josh Ramsay. 604 Records, 2015. Available at https://www.youtube.com/watch?v=jx9LC2kyfcQ Note - While I would love to take credit for this phrase, the credit is due to the band Marianas Trench for the use of this phrase in their song 'Astoria'.

11. Schroeder, Christa. *I was Hilter's Secretary*. The Telegraph, April 26, 2009. See https://www.telegraph.co.uk/culture/books/booknews/5201025/I-was-Hitlers-secretary.html

12. Schlesinger, Arthur. *Nothing Stands Still.* Cambridge, Mass.: The Belknap Press of Harvard University Press, 1969. The Lose Meaning of 'The Pursuit of Happiness", p. 95.

13. Ibid.

14. Conklin , Carli. *The Origins of the Pursuit of Happiness,* 7 Wash. U. Jur. Rev. 195 (2015). Available at: https://openscholarship.wustl.edu/law_jurisprudence/vol7/iss2/6

15. Ibid. See footnote 17.

Made in United States
Troutdale, OR
12/06/2024

26018654R00135